Winter 1985

Todd's body was rigid with fear caused by the insecurity of being left to face the unknown alone. His thin frame was convulsed with his sobbing. I tried to walk with him; finally I settled into my favorite, old rocking chair beside Robin's bed and gently rocked. Gradually, his twisted body relaxed and nestled closer as I rocked and purred soft nonsense into his ear.

We went on rocking, and all the while his brown eyes looked up at me. "How would you like a little milk?" I asked. I didn't expect an answer, but he nodded vigorously. I placed him in his bed and went to the kitchen to prepare a bottle.

I heard the school bus stop out front. Sue appeared first at the door. "Oh, Mommy!" she cried as her eyes settled on Todd. She rushed to the chair and knelt beside us. "You did take him! You did take him!"

ALL GOD'S CHILDREN

DOROTHY GAUCHAT

With a Foreword by Dorothy Day

BALLANTINE BOOKS • NEW YORK

Library of Congress Catalog Card Number: 75-20904

ISBN 0-345-31988-5

This edition published by arrangement with Hawthorn Books, Inc.

Manufactured in the United States of America

First Ballantine Books/Epiphany Edition: January 1985

Dedication

This book is dedicated, with all my love, to my husband, Bill. His burning love for others and stubborn clinging to high ideals blossomed forth in a life of sharing his talents and treasures with others—especially with me, our children, and God's children: the poor, the wounded, the handicapped.

He was a man of peace. By nature he was quiet and sometimes shy, except when others were unjustly treated. Then this small-statured man became an impassioned warrior. A poet and writer, he gave way to his dreams. His name should appear as co-author of this book. It was he who advised me, both of us working together on the first eighteen chapters, until his terminal illness took complete hold of him.

The children of Our Lady of the Wayside, especially the older ones, are no strangers to death. They have questioned, in their innate candor, the passing of their small companions and learned that they have gone home to God, their good and loving Father. They have given, and they have received the joy and the hope of the Mass of Resurrection; indeed, the presence of those little ones who have gone before us is almost tangibly felt. And so it came as no surprise when I told them that Poppi, as the children called Bill, had died, little Sue danced about and clapped her hands, shouting, "Oh goody, he's gone home to God!"

All of Bill's life and the work that we did together were inspired by the philosophy of "personal responsibility," which we learned from Dorothy Day and Peter

Maurin. After Bill's death, I discovered one of his last writings.

> *Bereft of its fleshly habitation in death*
> *the soul goes forth—a kind of birth.*
> *The process of dying has its evening*
> *sickness, the pangs of tearing loose.*
>
> *The spirit in its life period with the body*
> *has developed some of its potentialities to a*
> *greater or less degree, or in many has remained*
> *dormant—the straw men: too informed to be*
> *damned or be loved.*
>
> *As for me, may God see my retardation*
> *and remember my own feeble love for the*
> *wounded and handicapped.*

Contents

Foreword

What can I say about this book—the product of joint efforts by my friends William and Dorothy Gauchat? First of all, I can say that it kept me in on a beautiful spring day, utterly absorbed, so that I could not put it down until I had finished the last page. It was a beautiful view I had from my room at the farm at Tivoli, buds red on the maple tree outside, sun glistening on dancing waves of the river; the beauty of the book I was engrossed in matched the beauty outside. It is a story of a family who, in addition to their own children, take in one by one the saddest, most hopeless, most incurable of crippled children—spastics, brain-damaged, some victims of what courts call child abuse. The Gauchats make the picture one of strange beauty because of their faith, hope, and love.

During World War II, I visited conscientious objectors in a hospital for exceptional children. They served for four years, twelve hours a day, six days a week. The cutting off of government funds meant that tiny children were starving, filthy, and naked for want of the basic care a more adequate staff could provide. Millions of people have since seen the terrible sights of the wards in vast hospitals for the retarded.

This story is a picture of what could be done. It is a story of the courage, the cheerfulness, even the delight (one calls to mind Ruskin's phrase "the duty of delight") which can be a part of a life of dedicated service, such as the Gauchats'.

I have visited Dorothy and Bill many times and in many seasons and have seen Christmas celebrated around the tree, with everyone participating. I've seen the beauty of the sunny little lake, where the healthy Gauchat children shared in the care of the little ones, but I did not know of the annual visit to the amusement park with its Ferris wheels, roller coasters, and carnival atmosphere, which is described so delightfully, or of the ball game they went to. There is the exciting story of the flood which disrupts their small home. Also included are tragic accounts of the visits to state schools and institutions; these are heartrending. Such glimpses of the neglect and unbearable suffering of little children forced Ivan Karamazov to reject the harmony Christ died to bring.

One of the rules of Mother Theresa of India is that the sisters pick up the children and hug them as they pass through the wards of their foundling home in Calcutta. Dorothy Gauchat, as she was showing me through the new home for thirty-five children, was doing the same act instinctively. Love must be incarnate.

"Unless you become as little children . . ." There is the same savor of all this in the Gauchat book—the warmth of caresses, the emphasis on the comforts of food, warmth, and color, the thrill of children's games and excursions. How important this poor flesh of ours is; doomed for all of us to decay and suffer, and yet the source of delight!

The Gauchats know every facet of human suffering. I have often remembered, when I think of their own brain-damaged child and Bill's terminal illness, what Bill said to me once: "I have understood what Bernanos was getting at in his terrible book *Joy*." And as St. Augustine in his final conversation with Monica, at Ostia, pointed out—such understanding is a glimpse of heaven— the Beatific Vision.

DOROTHY DAY

～1～
The First Charge

He can't see—he is blind.
He can't hear—he is deaf.
He can't feel—he is atrophied.

Bill and I silently sat in the hospital, listening to a nurse as she prepared baby David—not our baby but somebody else's—for us to take home. Her competent, informed voice continued its instructions as she diapered and clothed the child and bundled him in blankets. "He is hydrocephalic, too; has severe water pressure on the brain. And there is lesion of the spine—spina bifida."

We could see the lump on the little back—a lump the size of a baseball, soft as a partly-inflated balloon. Even more distressing, indeed, shocking, was the size of the infant's head. It was as big as all the rest of him, heavy and difficult to handle. David's body, in comparison, seemed slight. It was as though his body was loosely suspended from the head.

We accepted the baby boy—six months of complications since birth—as the nurse handed him to us. We carried him outside to our parked automobile.

Bill started the engine and turned in the direction of home, where our beautiful, normal, three little girls waited for their first glimpse of their new brother.

How had we ever got ourselves into this sort of thing? What on earth had caused us to agree to care for this poor, hopeless creature? If asked, we would have been forced to answer, "Nothing on *earth*."

Often I have wondered about us. Had I been crazy to marry Bill—a man who had come out of college and opened a hospitality house? He was host, day and night, to drifting, jobless men, their clothing often infested, who came in for a bowl of soup and a place to sit—and sit. Bill never refused anyone help; how could he refuse a six-month-old baby?

Well, if we were crazy, we were crazy together.

Our first glimpse of each other—Bill and I—had been in the depth of the Great Depression when, with a couple of girls from the academy I was attending, I visited Bill's hospitality house. Once an abandoned store which the pigeons had taken over, it had been made into a haven for the unfortunates who roamed the city.

The house was in the midst of an area of broken-down houses where half-naked children—some naked from the waist up, some from the waist down—played in littered yards and stared at the passersby.

The youngsters along the street called Bill Mister Soup Man. At first the neighbors had been suspicious and antagonistic at the thought of somebody "attracting bums" to the neighborhood. Gradually they had changed; they came to lend a hand with cooking and cleaning and to share what they could with hungry men.

People thereabouts depended on Bill: "Bill, my kid's sick. Will you call the city doc? He don't pay no attention to me."; "Bill, my boy is in the workhouse, can you get him out?"; "Bill, will you talk to the relief people for us?"

We, my friends and I, grew interested. Our hearts were touched. We returned to help as best we could.

One day Bill asked, "Would you like to take some food and clothing to a family?" That's how we made the acquaintance of the Martins and in particular little Herbert Hoover Martin.

Walking toward the address we had been given, we chattered and felt strangely adventurous and important; one of us carried a box of clothing, another a bag of rolls and bread, and I held a long, slippery, smelly fish—I who had always disliked, if not detested, fish.

The home of the numerous Martin family was on the side of a hill, precariously suspended above the valley with its maze of railroad tracks and twisting, oil-slicked river.

Mrs. Martin opened the door, and we went in. We stood in a chilly, drafty room. Newspapers were stuffed in cracks in the walls. Two broken windows had been covered with cardboard. In a double bed, there was a barefoot baby and an assortment of cats, to protect the infant from rats, we learned. Another room, windowless, held a coal-burning kitchen range and a kerosene lamp.

The baby was Herbert Hoover Martin. The parents, we thought, must have been mighty faithful Republicans to name a child after the president in whose administration the depression had spread like a pall across the land.

Mrs. Martin was fingering through the box of clothing, wondering whether it might contain a pair of shoes for Herbert Hoover. "My husband's WPA check won't stretch very far," she said wistfully.

We looked at Herbert Hoover and at one another; we counted our resources—$1.62. We bundled little Herbert in a blanket smelling of coal oil and set off for a nearby store. In the dingy display window was a pair of baby shoes—$1.49.

"They don't come any cheaper," said the clerk. He spoke with no emotion, flatly. The depression had worn him down as it was wearing down everyone.

We counted out the $1.49 and fitted the little Herbert Hoover feet into the new shoes.

Bill and I were crazy to marry each other—no doubt about that. Some people were saying that the way the country was going, anybody was crazy to marry anybody and bring children into the world. But young people are forever optimistic, always adventurous. So, like countless other couples, Bill and I joined hands and hearts—"for better for worse, for richer for poorer, in sickness and in health, until death."

So there we were, a few years later, with three children—three girls; normal, healthy, lovely youngsters. Anita, the busy practical one, was small and wiry, with brown braids bouncing as she flew here and there, issuing orders, thinking up games to play. Helenmarie had golden hair, blue eyes, a dreamy disposition, and a bottomless store of questions with which to tax her parents' patience. And Suzie, the littlest one, had blue eyes, brown hair, and a playful nature.

One cold dawn I was awakened by the ringing of the telephone, and when I answered a sweet voice introduced itself as Sister Mary Somebody-or-other. She said that years ago she had had Bill in one of her classes. With that handle she started to twist my conscience. Would I take a handicapped baby to care for? Then, quickly, "It will be only for a short time. David is six months old and has been in a hospital since birth. The doctors didn't expect him to live even this long. Hydrocephalic . . . water on the brain, you know."

I didn't know, and I didn't want to know. I protested that I had three of my own to watch over. I said I knew nothing about caring for an ailing child.

The sister's voice became more and more soothing and yet, more and more gently insistent. "All David needs is to be kept clean and turned from one side to the other now and then. He may not live more than a week. At the most a month, the doctors say. It would be a great act of charity to take him."

The arm of my conscience was being twisted, twisted, twisted by that soft voice.

I said I'd think about it. I'd talk about it with Bill (Bill who had got me into this situation by taking in homeless and hopeless men).

Anita and Helenmarie had heard me on the phone. They wanted to know who had called so early in the morning. Little by little they wormed it out of me—Sister Mary So-and-so wanted us to take care of a baby boy.

Their voices rose in excitement and insistence, like the voices of youngsters when they're trying to talk their parents into letting them have a dog or a kitten. "Can we, mom! Can we have a baby brother?"

I told them the baby was sick. Immediately, Anita argued that I took good care of them when they were sick.

The baby's head was hurt, I told them. All the more reason for somebody to take care of him, was the upshot of their arguments.

Suddenly the thought overwhelmed me that we were talking about a person, an individual, one of God's immortal creations: hurt, yes; sick, yes; hopelessly handicapped, yes; but immortal.

The girls were pelting me with the arguments that children always use when they want to take in a stray pet. They'd help take care of him. He'd be no trouble. They'd watch over him. They meant what they were saying, but they were children, and children's memories are short about promises. Enthusiasm soon runs out, like the sands in an hourglass.

When I talked with Bill about it, he said matter-of-factly that it would be good to have a boy in the house. He helped me in digging a crib out of a storage room. We scrubbed it, and assembled rubber sheets, blankets, diapers, nursing bottles.

So now, here we were, homebound with poor little David. The nurse's recital was going through my head:

> He can't see—he is blind.
> He can't hear—he is deaf.
> He can't feel—he's atrophied.

Bosh. Next morning as I bathed David and rubbed talcum powder on his little body, I felt sure he heard my voice as I talked to him and felt the touch of my hands.

That evening, Bill sat at the crib talking and moving a bright toy back and forth above the eyes which seemed so tiny in the great head. And suddenly Bill said, "Dorothy, this kid can see!"

Helplessness calls forth love; and soon we all loved David. The children discovered, to their delight, that little chuckles came from him when they played around him and touched him.

"He can't see—he is blind." But he wasn't blind; he could see. "He can't hear—he is deaf." But he wasn't deaf; he could hear. His little hands were astonishingly strong, and he liked to have the children put toys in them so that he could toss them half-way across the room.

His little chuckles grew into laughter. His hair became

a halo of golden curls as we brushed and combed. We had a son; and our girls had a brother.

One day David wouldn't take his bottle. He drifted into a coma and made faint wails. His temperature rose to 105° Fahrenheit.

We notified the parents. "Probably it's the end," we said.

We phoned the doctor. "Isn't he a mess?" he said. He didn't know how heartless he sounded. David, to him, had never been a person.

To our surprise, David recovered; and as before, he could see, he could hear, he could laugh, and he could feel love. In some mysterious way, he communicated love; he returned love for love.

On a June day ("what is so rare?"), David's parents came and took him home with them. A strange emptiness was left in our house, relieved only by a host of memories. "Remember how David used to laugh when Daddy came home and talked to him? . . . Remember how he liked that tattered old teddy bear? . . . Remember how far he could throw that little doll of Helenmarie's?"

Even now it is hard to believe that six months later, when we saw David again, this time with his father and mother, he had begun to learn to talk.

~ 2 ~
Shadow of Fear

A year after David left us, Colette, our fourth child, was born. Never before while awaiting a birth had I considered the possibility that the baby might have some abnormality. I had vaguely prayed during previous pregnancies that all would be well, that the infant would be healthy and normal. But my mind had never conceived that an abnormal baby, such as David, existed.

Society, it seemed, for obscure reasons of shame or guilt, hid such unhappy incidents in a conspiracy of silence. But such thoughts and vague premonitions, like cloud shadows, did cross my mind during this pregnancy.

Colette was born in March. Tears of relief and gratitude flowed freely when the nurse brought her to me for the first time. She was perfect, all seven pounds of her; a lovely baby with delicate features framed in soft, wavy, brown hair.

In the following weeks, Colette did all the things babies of that age do. We enjoyed her. A healthy, happy baby is a joy, and some of the ache for David diminished.

Colette grew into an engaging youngster with cameo features and deliberate manners. She was somewhat on the quiet side—or perhaps she only seemed so because Sue, her predecessor as youngest, was so rollicking and rambunctious.

Eighteen months after Colette came Eric, our first son. He arrived on the Fourth of July, big, blond, blue-eyed, and full of bounce.

Colette, though quiet, was born with an insatiable curiosity. With each added year and the wonder of life around her, she asked endless questions. "What makes

7

fire dance?'' ''Why don't we have eyes in the back of our heads?''

One evening a serious discussion arose about creation and God. Eric, now five years old, asked, ''Where were we before we were born?'' As the older girls pondered, Colette answered, ''In the mind of God.''

One spring day she took part in an impromptu baseball game with her sisters and their friends of the pigtail set. There were the usual shrieks of girls at play. Then suddenly there was a strange silence. ''Something's wrong,'' I thought, and the girls burst into the house crying, ''Colette's hurt—hit by the bat.''

I bolted outdoors and saw her lying crumpled—a ball of clothing on the lawn. From a cut above her left eye, blood was streaming. As I picked her up, I could hear behind me a trembling voice asking, ''Is she dead?''

After applying a cold compress to her head, I drove her to the hospital. An intern stitched and bandaged the wound and sent us on our way after prescribing aspirin and smiling away any need for an X-ray examination. ''There's no cause for worry.

Gradually we began to notice that Colette did not always hear us. In the absentminded manner of parents, our reactions were traced with annoyance: ''Colette, please don't dawdle. Please listen to me when I speak to you.''

One day Eric and Colette were playing in the living room, and I called them for lunch. From the kitchen I could see toys scattered all over the floor. ''No lunch until you clean up,'' I warned. Then I heard Eric scolding Colette, ''Come on, help me, or I'm going to tell mommy.''

When I entered the room to referee the quarrel, Colette looked at me puzzled at being rebuked. ''I didn't hear you,'' she tried to explain as she set to work gathering up toys.

Another time, Bill took the children with him to the store. Walking along, Colette stopped and appeared to be looking back at something in the distance. Bill called her, but she ignored him.

''I didn't hear you,'' she said later.

One day, as was a custom, I read the children a story

after lunch. When I finished, they all took off in different directions to play, but Colette stood and stared into a corner of the room. "Story's over, Colette—run along and play," I coaxed. But she stood and stared, and suddenly I knew something was seriously wrong. I was afraid. I passed my hand up and down before her eyes. She seemed not to notice.

I couldn't get to the phone fast enough to call the doctor. He told me to calm down. "It's probably nothing serious," he assured me with professional confidence. "Bring her to the office this evening."

After his examination, during which he witnessed one of the staring episodes, he advised us to take Colette to a neurologist. We felt stunned at the frightening implications. A long series of tests, X-rays, and examinations by skilled practitioners and electronic machines led to the diagnosis: scar tissue on the left hemisphere of the brain.

The prognosis could only be deduced from a slight, deprecatory shrug of a neurologist's shoulders, since the treatment would be experimenting with various drugs. But before the trial-and-error therapy with drugs had fairly begun, it had to be postponed. Colette came down with whooping cough and mumps, no doubt picked up in a medical waiting room. For many weeks she was very ill. Then pneumonia developed, and the doctor detected symptoms of encephalitis. He made immediate arrangements for Colette to be admitted to the Isolation Ward of Metropolitan Hospital.

Colette's condition was critical through the first week, which she spent in an oxygen tent. The doctors observed her periodic dazes; these seemed to increase in frequency and duration as she convalesced. As her strength returned, she was given a wide variety of medication. Nothing helped; Colette began falling unconscious without warning. She became irritable and unhappy.

This period seems, in retrospect, a blurred montage: Colette with her head swathed in bandages from falls; doctors talking to us in hospital corridors, pointing out the pros and cons of brain surgery. In the end all agreed that nothing could be done. "Perhaps," they said, "some day a new drug, or a new technique in surgery . . ."

Each day brought deprivation, a denial of normal childhood activity for Colette, who kept whatever pain this caused her to herself. Bill and I tried to carry our anguish in a like manner.

Bike riding was a forbidden pleasure, as was splashing and wading in the creek. And hiking up the highway to the village store was hazardous enough for any child—Colette could only sit on the porch steps and watch as the other children set out. Usually they promised to bring back a treat for her; she would sit patiently waiting, thinking thoughts which only the good Lord knew.

Picnics at the amusement park were occasions when Colette was denied the thrills of the high rides, which she dearly loved. We shared the dejection her eyes expressed.

I didn't consider myself a parent of a handicapped child. Colette looked perfectly normal—still the pretty little girl with long brown braids. The doctors were vague, and they always said some drugs would help, or she would outgrow the illness.

When I asked, "Could it get worse?" a doctor would shrug and say, yes, that too was a possibility.

Imperceptibly, sorrow built a bridge and brought me an awareness and compassion with parents whose children suffer. I thought of David and knew in some degree what his mother had felt when he was stared at and rejected because he was different. This was happening to my daughter; if she fell on the sidewalk, as she sometimes did, people stopped and shot questioning glances at me. I wanted to cry out that she was fine; it was nothing serious, no more than a fainting spell. The people who stared did not understand; they did not know how to act, how to help, how to love.

My whole being wanted everyone to know Colette and to accept and love her. I felt outraged when they didn't, although I sensed that most people meant well. They would give generously to aid an unfortunate child—in a foreign land or in an orphanage. They would donate to the March of Dimes, to Christmas Seals, to United Appeals, to Easter Seals—but they were at a loss how to speak, to smile, to be friendly and at ease with a handicapped child.

They saw only the handicap, and it blocked their view of the child. They did not realize that such children are more normal than abnormal and want to be accepted exactly as are their peers who have no handicaps.

An illuminating incident occurred during one of Colette's frequent hospital stays. She was so happy that particular day; she soon revealed the cause of her high spirits. My usually quiet little girl said, "Oh, mommy, I have the nicest friend here. You'll meet her this afternoon."

"But, honey, you have many friends here, the doctors, nurses, all the children."

She shook her head. "They're nice, but not my friends. This lady stops to visit and talk with me. You'll see."

After hearing the swishing of a mop and the rattle of a bucket, I saw a wide, generous smile on the face of a woman in a blue and white uniform; she was short and on the plump side. Her sparkling merry eyes made me feel good, as if happiness was the normal human condition. She was Colette's friend Bertha.

"Hi, Colette," she said. "How's my girl today?"

Colette responded with a torrent of words, introducing me and telling her about a radio program she liked. It was an effort for me to restrain my tears.

Later, in the hall Bertha told me about her chats with Colette, and how she had picked her up one day when she dropped unconscious.

This woman, with her simple wisdom, had the perception to conceal any alarm, curiosity, or pity in Colette's presence. She had the insight needed to see the whole personality of the stricken child. While not denying Colette's handicap, she placed it in proper perspective, speaking casually about it in Colette's presence, along with all the amusing anecdotes and hospital gossip that were interesting to junior patients. Colette responded and clung to this genuine, unassuming, matter-of-fact love.

My heart was filled with gratitude for this woman, who loved my daughter for what she was—a little girl with a handicap. She had learned to know her and knowing her, loved her.

Two years of weekly trips to the clinic, where neurologists examined Colette, asked questions, and prescribed drugs, brought no improvement. Our anguish of uncertainty remained unrelieved. Then suddenly, completely, the blackouts stopped, "a total remission of symptoms," a doctor said.

For a while we thought we had just missed seeing Colette in a spell. But weeks of observation confirmed our unspoken hope; she was well.

Our little-girl-lost was home again. She rejoined her sisters and brothers in their activities and games; she climbed the high sliding boards and was again a member of the trapeze act in the barn circus, swinging from beam to beam on the ropes in the hayloft.

The shadow of fear of the unknown walked our home no more.

~ 3 ~
Our House

The locale of our memories was our small house. My father, a skilled craftsman in wood, eloquently conveyed his opinion that it was poorly designed, badly built, a frightful example of shoemaker carpentry by a studied silence. But as any do-it-yourselfer knows, your first house is not always perfect. And there was one aspect of our house which, beyond any quibble, was beautiful: it had no shadow of a mortgage.

It was put together from parts of a portable schoolhouse. It had high ceilings and big windows, facing south. The ceilings were painted a true blue to lower them, and the walls were light gray.

Some of our talented friends designed colorful murals on inviting spaces of the walls; there was a St. William, abbot, and a St. Dorothy with a basket of green apples. In the kitchen-dining area was a brush-lettered "Pater and Ave" in reds and blues with vine tracery around them—reminiscent of pages of an illuminated manuscript Book of the Hours.

We papered parts of one wall with maps of the world, of America, and of Newport, Rhode Island, where I had lived and studied for a year, and where we married. These preserved many happy memories and were also excellent for teaching geography.

There came a time, though, when the walls seemed to shrink and close in on us; our family was growing. Our second son, David, was a year old—named for the foster son of years before, who had died. We were outgrowing the home which had been a living part of us. It possessed a worth only we could appreciate; the fireplace

13

Bill had made from stone gathered on the farm, the
wood carvings and paintings from our early artsy-craftsy
days, and the built-in bookshelves that lined our living
room walls.

It was the kind of house where sitting on the floor
with the children seemed the natural thing to do. Discussions of ideals and dreams and taking turns drawing in a
sketchbook and improvising verse created:

> *Tell, me pretty butterfly*
> *Why you flutter while you fly?*
>
> *Tell me, while you flutter by*
> *Why they call you butterfly?*
>
> *I can see*
> *Why they call a honeybee*
> *Cuz they give us honey, free.*
>
> *But to call you butterfly*
> *Seems to be an utter lie!*
>
> *They should call you Flutterfly*
> *You don't give us butter, fly,*
>
> *Cuz*
> *Cows duz!*

That verse inspired drawings of flying cows and butterflies with pails. Another epic the children loved was one
that went like this:

> *Every time you say your prayers*
> *You are climbing golden stairs.*
>
> *And a lot of praying brings*
> *A pair of sprouting angel wings.*
>
> *For Jesus loves the weak and small*
> *May he bless you one and all.*

Doggerel, certainly, but our doggerel, and it was illus-
trated with pictures of funny little angels climbing the
stairs, one angel to a stair, to infinity—or to the top of
the page anyway.

There were always visitors; some came for a brief visit, others stayed and stayed, and there were children from the city who came for vacation. Our small Suzie, whenever she spied a stranger coming up the drive, grew jubilant with excitement. Once she ran into the house crying out, "Mommy, mommy, we have company! There's a man here with his suitcase!" Sure enough, it was a visitor with a suitcase—a Fuller brush salesman.

Across the road from us was a hundred-year-old red brick house. This, we were told, was the original farmhouse of our farm, but years ago it had been sold separately with five acres. For a century it had been a landmark, with its high slate roof, its white gables, and a square tower rising up to a sharp copper finial. It stood among tall trees—maple, horse chestnut, and one very old gingko, a rarity.

Often we had admired the house, solid against a sinking sun, a lovely view from our windows. Through the years, we saw a variety of tenants move in and out. The last one was, he said, "a doctor of naturopathy. Disease is only the result of selfish, destructive self-indulgence. I am a teacher, not a healer."

He called his home a health school and equipped rooms for twelve patients. He was constantly harassed by the State Medical Society, which finally caused him to move elsewhere. The house he left behind, with the For Sale sign on it, was a white elephant; for two years it remained empty.

Unexpectedly we had a buyer for our acreage, and when we received the first payment we wrote to the doctor and made an offer to buy his place. This was the beginning of a protracted correspondence that ended with us becoming the owners.

As we wrote to a friend: "Well, it was always the home we had dreamed of having, but never really believed that we could possibly ever get. It has about six acres of land, wooded and lawned, and a lovely lake in the back. We call it a lake although it isn't actually anything but a pond; but it is spring fed, and it's full of fish. The water is clear, and the kids love to swim in it."

With the aid of good friends, moving across the road was a family affair. Chairs were hoisted to a shoulder or

head and carried across. Even the small fry helped by
carrying a picture or a book.

It was a dark, November Saturday, and a heavy wet
snow was falling. The only big problem proved to be the
piano, an ancient upright, extremely heavy. We had just
about despaired of getting it on the pickup truck, after
much tugging and grunting; we lacked the little extra
vim. At this point a stranger appeared, a husky young
fellow; he wanted to know if he could buy the wheels
from an old haywagon he saw in the barnyard. Gladly,
we told him; he could have the wheels if he would give
us a hand with the piano, which he did. Soon the piano
was set up in its new home, and Anita could practice her
music lessons.

For days afterwards there were boxes to unpack and
curtains to be hung; the tasks seemed endless. In the
midst of all this wonderful chaos, Helenmarie came home
from school and announced that her class was present-
ing a program, and all the mothers were to come.

I thought I'd be excused. I didn't have the car at
home during the day; Colette, Eric, and David were
preschoolers, and babysitters were impossible to find.
But Helenmarie wasn't one to take no for an answer.
She arranged with one of her classmates to have her
mother drive all of us to school.

The day of the performance was cold and gray. But it
was a big day for Helenmarie, who was in the cast, and
for the little ones, who had never seen a play. My heart
wasn't in it, I wanted to stay home, unpack, get things
organized, and soak in the warm joy of being in our new
home.

I remember little of the program except that it was a
choral presentation. Helenmarie's skirt hung crooked,
and I was annoyed with myself for not checking her
over before she left for school that morning.

After a visit with the teachers to express our congratu-
lations on their splendid work with the children, we
headed for home at last. My mind was busily planning
the tasks I would do when suddenly Eric said to our
automobile hostess, "Won't you come to lunch at our
house? She can come to lunch, can't she, mommy?"

My heart skipped a beat. I could see all my plans

upset—and worse yet was the realization of how little food there was in the house to prepare lunch for this pleasant woman, a total stranger to us until that morning. But she laughed, accepted the invitation, and shared our scrambled eggs, doughnuts, and coffee. She was a warm and vivacious woman; she thrilled with me over the house as we showed her around.

After lunch the children disappeared to play, and we sat back relaxed. The conversation drifted to children, as it always does with young mothers. I told her about Colette and her recovery, and David, our first foster child.

Soon she was telling me of an aunt of hers who had been a foster mother to numerous children; she said there was a tremendous need for foster homes. She and her husband wanted to take in another child to add to their family of four but did not have the needed room.

After she left I couldn't get the vision of homeless children out of my mind. As I worked a thought kept recurring, "Surely we have room for more youngsters." At dinner that evening, I gave Bill a quick summary of my day and ended with the question, "What do you think about applying at Child Welfare for a foster child?"

"Don't you have enough work with six kids?"

"What's one more? And we have all this room. Above all, Colette is well—maybe we owe something for that."

It was agreed. I would call the welfare people the next day. That night, we talked much about our children, and about David, who was, by right of our discovery of his person and personality, so much our own. Suddenly we realized that we wanted to take a child no one else wanted—a handicapped child.

The next morning I called the Child Welfare Bureau. A social worker suggested that I come in for an interview; we agreed on December 8.

The skies that day were deep blue accented by swiftly moving cumulus clouds. It was cold, but the brightness of the sun made a glow of warmth inside. Many questions had to be answered: the size of our family, how long we had lived in our town, the size of our house, our income. I began to experience the devious indirection of

bureaucracy; my interviewer was puzzled when I speci-
fied a preference for a handicapped child. Briefly, I told
her the story of David; she nodded several times. Perhaps she understood. She closed the interview by promising to call me soon.

Two days later she phoned to say she had a baby to
place with us—a sick baby, difficult to handle; one who
cried almost constantly. He was recovering from pneumonia in a hospital and would probably be released in a
week. If we found him too difficult to care for, she
would understand.

He was nine months old. His name was Robin. This
was the child we were hoping for. While we waited, we
worked with new energy to get the house in order,
especially the nursery room. In medieval days a guest
room was known as the Christ-room; the ancient wisdom of a Gaelic rune said, "Often, often, often goes the
Christ in the stranger's guise."

Throughout the waiting days, the children talked and
talked about the new baby brother. They helped me to
arrange his room; they questioned me endlessly about
his damaged brain.

~ 4 ~
The False Accusation

Christmas that year was memorable. It was the first one in our new home, which had plenty of room in a windowed bay for the bushy Scotch pine we chose for the Yule tree. A special cause of joy was that Colette was well. And the new baby, Robin, was with us. The children bubbled with excitement and hung decorations on his crib for his delight.

Robin's parents and a social worker brought him to us. His pink face was wreathed with soft, wavy, brown hair and his big eyes, too, were a soft brown. He came wearing red overalls; he looked like his name.

At first glance he seemed like any other nine-month-old baby, but a closer look disclosed the differences. He was afflicted with total cerebral palsy. At times his body became so rigid that he could not make any voluntary movement; he was even unable to swallow his saliva.

He could not see, but he could hear; he communicated with throaty cooings to show his joy in existing and with a strangled wailing to express pain. When spoken to, he smiled. There was almost an aura about him; we always felt that he gave more to us than we ever gave to him.

His parents were very young but seemed, at the same time, old. His mother had been gravely ill; the marks of suffering were etched on her face. One wanted to reach out to her, to assure her that her baby would be fine, that we would love him as she did and make him happy and comfortable.

Robin cried much of the time, as his mother had said

he had from the first day. It seemed that he would continue to do so for all future time.

For several weeks we followed religiously the directions given regarding his diet. He was fed four times a day on milk and syrup, plus baby foods and medication prescribed to control seizures.

It was pathetic to see Robin struggle to suck the bottle. The prepared baby foods, though soft and smooth, gagged him. His stomach soon rejected the little he did swallow. I wondered whether all this effort and tension were causing colic which, in turn, triggered long periods of agonized crying. The doctor had no advice to offer; he assumed that a mother ought to know how to feed a baby.

I decided to do some experimenting. I tried spoon feeding, but it gagged him. I used an eyedropper; it was too slow. Finally, I cut a large hole in the nipple; it worked. He relaxed and enjoyed his bottle.

The success gave me a grand feeling of achievement. In the following days, I gradually included cereal, raw egg, and baby fruit and vegetables in his bottle. Later orange juice and soup were added. Robin's long crying jags stopped. Eureka!

But Robin was subject to sudden respiratory infections, some critical. These were caused by an inability to swallow. Saliva would clog his throat and enter his lungs.

The first such episode developed soon after his arrival. The physician who had cared for him refused to come to the house to see him. "He is a hopeless case," he told me over the telephone. "He'll never grow up to be a football player." To me, that seemed a classic non sequitur, but it is exactly what the doctor said.

We have learned, through the passing years, that few doctors seem to be willing to spend time on these "hopeless" kids. One pediatrician told us frankly that "doctors are just as helpless as parents with these children." If they don't know the answers, they can't help the parents; they dismiss the problem by advising parents to put the child away in an institution—advice that often has tragic effects on the parents.

A wise doctor, Walter C. Alvarez, has said, "Too often parents are left feeling terribly alone and outcast.

Lucky are those who find a doctor who senses their
sorrow and sympathizes; who handles their baby with
tenderness and is willing to stand by them and not leave
them all alone with their problems.''

This lack of concern by doctors didn't make sense to
me. I felt that children should have natural rights to
medical care, whether normal or abnormal. To an un-
complicated mind like mine, it seemed that an abnormal
child would have the greater need for expert care.

Robin was ill; he needed a physician. We called a
doctor who had just set up practice in the community.
He prescribed antibiotics and suggested that we elevate
the foot of the bed, keeping Robin on his stomach, with
a pillow underneath him. This would enable the saliva to
flow from his mouth; it proved effective and added greatly
to the child's comfort. It also added a mite to the minute
store of our practical knowledge of the care of a handicapped child. It encouraged us to improvise, to dare to
pioneer when new problems arose later.

Robin recovered rapidly from his illness. With his new
diet and his new sleeping position, he grew more con-
tented by the day. He seemed to enjoy the household
noise and bustle and the frequent visits from the youngsters. He was quick to respond with his wide, ecstatic
smile.

Music was a special treat for him; he cooed with
contentment to the strains of a Strauss waltz.

A few crocuses appeared on the front lawn one morning as purple proof that hard winter was melting into
spring. The children were getting restless, trying to rush
the season by shedding coats and caps, anxious to pack
school books away and plunge into vacation fun. Colette
continued in good health, and Robin's respiratory infections struck less frequently as his strength increased.

Usually I was the one who yawned my way through
the ritual of preparing breakfast and packing lunches for
father and children, who would appear somewhat later.
As always, I peeked in to see Robin first; his room was
just off the kitchen, where we could listen to him, and
he could hear the family activity. On this spring morning,
he was sleeping peacefully as I looked in at him.

After breakfast, when the older children had sped off

to school in their yellow bus, I went to Robin's room to feed him. I stiffened in horror: his face was blue, his breathing shallow.

A torrent of apprehension flooded my mind. How could this happen, he was fine a short while ago; what should I do? He seemed close to death. I prayed as I drew water for an alcohol bath; if this was the result of a convulsion, the bath might revive him.

I lost all conception of time: I called the doctor, he wasn't in; I dialed the police number for help to get the baby to the hospital. There was only one policeman on duty and he was out on a call.

Finally a neighbor helped me rush Robin to the hospital. I must have been in a state of shock; I felt so cold and weak in the car as it broke all speed limits. All this time Robin did not even seem to be struggling to breathe.

The nurse in the emergency room knew at a glance the urgency of the situation. She took the baby from my arms and rushed him to a stretcher with an oxygen unit beside it. I followed helplessly. There were others in the green-tiled room; I remember them as figures from a dream. When the nurse realized I was there, she ordered me from the room and closed the door. I sat on a wooden bench in the hall, dazed by the events that had swept me along since early morning. I whispered a prayer as hospital sounds and smells swirled around me. I could hear the hushed activity behind the doors of the emergency room. I was frightened. How could this happen so fast? He had been sleeping so peacefully such a short time before!

The door swung open and the nurse approached, and from the look on her face, I knew something terrible was wrong. She began asking questions about Robin. I explained that I was not his mother, but a foster mother; that my friend was calling Robin's mother, and when she arrived she could give the history herself.

"I don't want to see the mother. It's you I want to talk to," she said sharply. "Did you give this baby any kind of medication? What kind? How much?"

She shot questions at me. I answered as calmly as I could, giving the name of the medicine and the dosage. I said that I had given none that morning because of the condition he was in.

She looked at me coldly, saying, "To me it looks as if this baby has been given an overdose of medicine."

I was stunned. This unsmiling woman was saying that I had tried to kill Robin—or had killed him. I did not know if he was dead or alive.

The horror of her words, coupled with the suspicion in her eyes, left my mind numb; the sound and motion about me all seemed unreal. In this faraway state, I heard her say, "Follow me."

She led me into the emergency room where a doctor and a nurse were working with Robin, giving him artificial respiration and administering oxygen. Another doctor standing by was quietly saying over and over again: "Let him die gently."

This soft-spoken phrase kept sounding in my mind, echoing and reechoing— "Let him die gently,"—to which I kept answering, praying: "Dear God, let him live."

Shortly afterwards the nurse told me to leave the room again. I returned to my vigil in the hall. It was broken only by a hurried call to the social agency to notify them of Robin's admission to the hospital. I had no concept of time. Perhaps an hour passed before Robin was wheeled out, and a young intern came to tell me he would live.

I don't think I spoke a word to the doctor. I just sat on the bench, too drained to move. The accusation of the nurse was unbelievable, but it had happened. Suddenly I knew what it meant to be falsely accused. Her attitude and her words had convicted me of attempted murder, and I felt stained, somehow guilty.

I wanted nothing more than to get out of that hospital. I asked my neighbor, who had stayed patiently with me, to take me home. I didn't even want to see Robin. The doctor had said that he would live, and that was all that mattered. There was nothing I could do for him now.

~ 5 ~
Good-bye and Hello

Our ride home was in silence. My neighbor seemed to understand the spirit-draining ordeal I had been through. I slumped on the seat of the car, trying to relax despite the horrid events of the morning.

I wondered about the nurse; why had she been so quick to judge? Could it be that during her experience in the emergency room she had seen many children who had been given overdoses by parents?

It is true that children make daily newspapers by exploring medicine cabinets and swallowing what they find. But Robin was a helpless baby; surely she couldn't really think that I had dosed him deliberately.

I was a foster mother; foster parents want the children they care for. They need not keep them if they do not wish to do so.

Perhaps the nurse was ill herself, or overworked, or plagued by personal problems which she had to take out on someone. Whatever the reason, as a nurse she had no right to make such snap judgments; she hadn't behaved as a professional.

When we got home, it was hard to believe that so much time had elapsed. Slowly my anguish subsided and gave way to anger. My placid disposition was ready to explode. I wanted to return to the hospital to see the superintendent and supervisor of nurses, to complain about the kind of nurse they were employing.

Work was impossible. My stomach recoiled at the thought of lunch. Restlessly I wandered about the house, picking up, here and there, random articles that I dropped elsewhere, biding my time until Bill got home from work.

24

At three o'clock the school bus released the bundles of energy the driver knew as the Gauchat kids. They sped across the lawn, leaped to the porch, and raced through the door; dropping books on the kitchen table, they came to a stop between the breadbox and the refrigerator. With peanut butter and jelly sandwiches in hand, they marched to Robin's room and in unison asked "Where's Robin?"

I explained quietly that he had suddenly become ill and I had taken him to the hospital; but that he would be all right in a few days. The news seemed to take away their zest and appetite, and they slowly climbed the stairs to change school clothes for jeans and sneakers.

At five o'clock Bill arrived, and I unburdened my heavy and angry heart. He listened with a darkening silence. We had to postpone our discussion about what we would do until the children were in bed.

We were quiet that evening at dinner. Later, as the children were at their homework, I called the hospital and talked to the doctor who had treated Robin. He explained that mucus had clogged Robin's throat and choked him. He said he was responding well. Neither he nor I mentioned medication.

Much later that evening, over a cup of coffee at the kitchen table, I related (and relived) the story of my day; the sequence of events, my fears, actions, and anger; and now my fear of taking Robin back. The responsibility of a foster child loomed immense. After a long discussion we decided to give up Robin. It was a difficult and sad decision; we had grown to love him. Next morning I told the social worker. She urged me to take time to reconsider.

The one thing we had not reckoned with was the strong feelings of our children. They were heartbroken when we told them Robin would not be back. They begged us to keep him. We listened with increasing pride, love, and sadness.

At the end of the week, the social worker phoned to assure us that Family Service knew the good care we were giving Robin and had complete confidence in us. Between the pressures of our children and our own deep love for Robin, we decided in favor of another try.

There was great celebrating in our house that evening.

~ 6 ~
The Advent of Todd

Cool spring melted into hot summer. The children thrived in the sun and freedom from school. Our lake was always occupied with little people in bright colored swimsuits; the air was filled with the happy cries and shrieks of jumping, diving aquabelles and boys. Our yard always seemed to be filled with youngsters popping out from every tree and bush. There were extras for lunch and picnics. It was a happy time of the year.

Robin, with us again, improved in these hot months; his respiratory infections were less frequent, and his daily sunbaths on a chaise lounge turned him into a brownish-red Robin.

Visitors were frequent, too, and one who influenced the course of our lives was the county school nurse. Her first visit, no doubt, was in the line of duty, but thereafter her calls seemed the visits of a dear friend. She was a slim woman of medium height, who carried herself erect with professional pride in her blue uniform. Her eyes sparkled with friendship.

She loved children, especially those with special problems. She took a keen interest in Colette and Robin and came often to ask about their welfare. She would offer advice when asked but was careful not to impose her ideas.

One day she told us about a boy, two years old, who had cerebral palsy. He lived in a neighboring village. She was impressed with this little fellow's determination, expressed through his eyes and his patient, feeble attempts at moving about on the floor. She became animated as she described him.

"I wish you could meet him," she said. "I know you'd agree that some day he will walk across a stage on commencement night to get his diploma."

In late summer a young man came to our door carrying a small boy. He had heard that we had taken a handicapped child into our home, and he introduced us to his son, Todd. He explained to me and to the children, who had gathered around, that Todd had cerebral palsy. He needed a home.

Todd's parents were recently divorced, and the father had gained custody of Todd and his twin sister, Tolly, a normal child, who was being cared for by friends. He could not find a home for Todd; he asked us to take him.

Todd looked famished. One thought of the pictures of children in refugee camps. His arms and legs, pitifully thin, thrashed out uncontrollably. He was tiny (thirteen pounds) but he had the face of an older child.

One wanted to cry with pity. Then I saw his eyes. They were deep brown, brimming with intelligent interest. And he had a wholehearted smile as he looked at me. Suddenly, I realized that this was the child the county nurse had been telling me about.

Our children clustered about Todd as his father put him on the floor. He took in the strange surroundings and strange faces. He saw a newspaper across the room and set his jaw in determination. His body jerked and edged its way toward his goal. The children wanted to get the paper for him, but his father stopped them and told them to watch.

Todd was straining every muscle and nerve, but his face was aglow with challenge. He reached his goal, beads of perspiration covering his face and dampening his brown hair. I felt exhausted from watching him. He gurgled with glee, waving the crumpled paper like a flag of victory.

We were all caught up in the excitement of this diminutive hero's achievement. There was something contagious about his joyful determination. The children gathered about him on the floor, and Todd seemed to enjoy the attention. As they played, his father drew me aside and explained again his need for a home for Todd.

The thought of another child to care for seemed impossible. I explained about Robin, who took much time to feed and whose illnesses came without warning. It was a hard thing to turn the young man away; he seemed to have more than his share of heartaches.

The children frowned their disapproval at me. They wanted to keep Todd. A glow of gratitude spread over me. We were blessed with happy, generous kids. Their hearts and home were open to everybody and everything.

A week hardly passed when one didn't come home with an injured bird, a stray kitten, or a puppy. Our menagerie numbered nine cats, a dog, six puppies, and a hamster; later, rabbits and baby chicks were added. In the spring there was usually a box with an injured bird that David was trying to heal. Our pond was full of fish, and the first spring sport was fishing. David and Eric used a net and bread for bait; they always threw their catch back, but sometimes one of the cats would pounce on a fish, much to David's anguished dismay.

This same child love for God's creatures carried over into their love for our handicapped Robin; now I could see in their eyes the question: "Why can't we have another brother?"

Holding Todd in my lap, I could feel his ribs. He was pitifully thin. Yet, he possessed a hidden spring of vitality. For me it was love at first sight. My words of refusal to his father must have sounded hollow—as indeed they were.

As Bill's car came into the driveway that evening, the children raced to see who could reach him first. Reaching him first was important, because the lucky one had the floor and could reel off the big events of the day. First one was it, according to Bill's rules of order. Anita, the oldest, was the winner that evening. As their father extricated himself from the car—carefully so as not to step on anyone or anything—Anita announced the advent of Todd.

It's amazing how quickly children can give a rundown on news. "And daddy," she said, "we'll help mom take care of him. Please say we can have him." The others joined in the chorus of please.

To say Bill was a bit overwhelmed would be an understatement. He whispered to me, "It looks like another snow job."

We sat out under the stars, that evening, at the side of our little lake, where a hungry fish leaped up with a splash after some flying insect. I gave Bill the details of the day. My heart felt for Todd as the children's did. I tried to be realistic and practical about the boy, but in the face of human suffering and love, it is hard to be practical. I realized, after talking with Bill, that I wanted deeply to add Todd to our family.

~7~
An Obstacle Overcome

One of the things we lacked in our home was an adequate water supply. There was one shallow well of very hard water and a large cistern to hold rain water. In summer the well dried up, and the rains came too late and too little for our needs. More than once, I was in the midst of washing mounds of sorted clothing only to discover the automatic washer working through its appointed cycle with no water in it. Then there would be the long wait for a water truck to haul in a tankload (about 2,000 gallons), usually arriving late at night. Meanwhile, there were trips across the road to patient neighbors for refills of jugs of drinking water.

I was as frugal as possible in the use of water, as of everything else. I shopped for the children's clothes with an eye for materials that didn't show soil. But there remained Robin; his clothes had to be antiseptically clean, thoroughly rinsed to avoid the risk of bed sores.

That particular problem was solved in the yellow pages of the telephone book which listed laundries. I called the closest one, and arranged for diaper service. The diaper problem was solved, leaving only the light chore of folding and sorting. As I was doing that one afternoon, thoughts of Todd occupied my mind. I told myself again that perhaps I could manage another child. With the laundry under control a big part of the work was taken care of; I had also heard of a woman in the village who did day work. Perhaps, if I had her come a day or two, I would have time for another child. Besides, our girls were a big help with dishes and in caring for their rooms.

Why I persisted in mulling over these plans, God

knows, not I. When I told Bill, he reminded me that I had already told Todd's father that I could not care for him. Probably the little fellow was safely settled in a new home. The incident was closed.

The days were growing shorter. The children had returned to school, and the sounds and smells of autumn were in the air. The house had taken on a comparative quietness and a new order; a schedule had to be met, for school buses wait for no laggard scholar. Homework occupied the early evening hours; the freedom of summer was over.

One evening as the children were gathered around the table in the kitchen, working at school assignments, the telephone bell rang and disturbed the industrious silence. I did not recognize the voice of the caller until he mentioned Todd.

"Do you think you could reconsider taking Todd? I haven't been able to find a home for him."

"Let me discuss it with my husband. I'll call you back tomorrow."

A telephone call was still a big event in our family. Everyone was watching as I ended the conversation. "Just a salesman," I fibbed. To Bill I said, "How about a quick walk around the yard? It's a beautiful night and a beautiful moon."

"As soon as I get my pipe," he answered.

The children settled back resignedly to their books. As we went out the door, we reminded them that we would be close to the house and there was to be no fooling around. We walked through the dried leaves. Bill took a long time lighting his pipe, waiting for me to begin.

"It was Todd's father," I said finally. "He can't find a home for him. He wants to know if we would take Todd."

Bill softly hummed *Que Sera Sera* as I talked. "You know the children have the right idea," he said, "the right spirit, the Christian spirit of hospitality. Remember how at the hospitality house, we welcomed everyone? At first the neighbors complained about the bums and tramps, and the police sent city health inspectors who complained about the chipped cups and cracked bowls."

"And," I said, "you told them a hungry man was kept from starvation by what was in the cracked and chipped dishes."

"Right, let's keep up the spirit of hospitality. We'll take Todd."

We shared a quiet smile. In the October moonlight it was settled. We decided not to tell the children; we'd surprise them.

It was a brilliant October day when Todd arrived. The warm sun brought out the vibrant fires of the oaks, maples, white ash, and other trees; the sky was deep blue and hung with a few, white cloud puffs. A drowsy hazy blue was on the horizon.

For Todd, I'm afraid, it wasn't a happy day. As his father assembled his bed, he watched with apprehension. He was frightened. He didn't want to come to me. He lay on the floor close to his father.

He looked pitiful and scrawny; his head was bald in patches. Evidently someone had attempted to give him a haircut. Doing that for a spastic child is an unnerving undertaking, we later learned by experience.

Upon finishing the work on the bed, Todd's father lifted him in his arms and settled down in a big chair. Quietly he tried to explain to the boy why he was leaving him with a new family. He had to return to work and Todd couldn't be left alone. He promised to visit him often; Todd tried to accept this, fighting back tears, but it was too much. He buried his small head on his father's chest and sobbed in utter misery.

I motioned to his father to give him to me. "Perhaps," I said, "it would be best to leave. It will take a little time for him to adjust."

Todd's body was rigid with fear caused by the insecurity of being left to face the unknown alone. His thin frame was convulsed with his sobbing. I tried to walk with him; finally I settled into my favorite, old rocking chair beside Robin's bed and gently rocked. Gradually, his twisted body relaxed and nestled closer as I rocked and purred soft nonsense into his ear.

We went on rocking, and all the while his brown eyes looked up at me. "How would you like a little milk?" I asked. I didn't expect an answer (I suppose I was almost as frightened as he), but he nodded vigorously. I placed him in his bed and went to the kitchen to prepare a bottle.

His father had said he could drink from a bottle but had difficulty with it, and he also had problems with solid foods. (We learned gradually that he had a reversed eating pattern. What went into his mouth did not always stay there; a sudden spasm rejected the food, and we had to start over again. But he loved food, and any sight or mention of it brought him to full attention.) With the warmed bottle in my hand, Todd and I resumed our rocking. Now his hungry mouth grabbed the nipple. He choked and sputtered. Milk dribbled from the side of his mouth. It was painful to watch his hungry effort; he'd stop momentarily to catch his breath, though he seemed fearful that I might take the bottle from him. I felt myself growing tense and exhausted along with him. It was an empathy that was to flourish later and needed no words for communication.

It was hard to imagine anyone so hungry—and so helpless to meet the need. I realized how much we take for granted—walking, talking, eating, drinking, relaxing; this child could do none of these ordinary, natural things.

As I was pondering this, Todd swallowed the last drop of milk and slumped exhausted in my arms. Sweat ran down his forehead and cheeks.

I heard the school bus stop out front. Sue appeared first at the door. "Oh mommy!" she cried as her eyes settled on Todd. She rushed to the chair and knelt beside us. "You did take him! You did take him!"

~ 8 ~
Acceptance

As weeks passed swiftly, tranquilly, Todd's bony body filled out; his skin took on a bronze glow, replacing the aged, dehydrated pallor of a malnourished child. The long hours of patience with him were showing results. His older sisters were proud of their skill in feeding him. Love, as much as the food in his bottle, were needed to get nourishment into that shrunken body.

The cerebral palsy (athetoid type) affected the upper part of Todd's body; hence, he could not control the movement of his arms and could not balance his body in a sitting position. His head jerked, and the muscles of his throat involuntarily constricted, making it impossible for him to swallow until the muscles relaxed. Although he never became discouraged as he slurped, he did become exhausted. Often after this intense struggle, he fell asleep in our arms, his clothing damp with perspiration.

He seemed to be chronically hungry, always on the lookout for an extra snack. He spent hours with us in the kitchen—the center of the house—watching the family in action. He sat in a narrow chair designed for spastics; it could be tilted back to keep his body from falling forwards. It had been given to him by the local Cerebral Palsy Society.

As I prepared meals, Todd would open his mouth wide, like a young bird in its nest; when I held a spoon and medicine bottle for Robin, Todd opened for a share of it. Underneath these amusing antics, one sensed the chill memory of the hunger that he and millions of other children the world over suffer.

We added eggs and honey to whole milk to give him

35

as much nourishment as possible. Not only did his body thrive, but his damaged spirit mended.

He suffered nightmares in the first months. He would wake up crying uncontrollably as he crouched in a corner of his crib with his head buried in the bedclothes, like an abused puppy hiding from tormentors. We did not know what experience had caused such terrible fear, nor did we wish to know.

The response of our younger son, David, to his new brother was a joy to watch. David (four at that time) was a sensitive boy—a born naturalist, who would nurse a sick cat to health and shed tears of rage at the same creature for doing what comes naturally, killing a bird.

After asking endless questions about Todd's condition, David accepted the difference and adopted Todd as his playmate. The two spent hours on the living room floor playing with trucks and trains, building forts, and having noisy, make-believe battles. David had an uncanny way of communicating with Todd. There was immediate understanding and rapport between them. If Todd couldn't handle a toy, David did it for him; he was quick to notice Todd's needs.

At other times, Todd was content to spend long hours watching David working on his "projects," as he called them. He loved to draw and make things, even at this early age; he had a flair for creative crafts. Todd was content watching castles form out of cardboard cartons and polished tin cans. He didn't seem to mind that he couldn't use his hands to join in but sat back, his eyes glowing with admiration at David's triumphs.

Todd had been with us five months when the county nurse, who had introduced him to us, made arrangements at the outpatient clinic of a nearby orthopedic hospital to have him examined. It was a cold day in March. The halls of the outpatient department were lined with wooden benches. There the mothers sat, each one holding her broken child. Some of the little patients were in wheelchairs, some struggled about on crutches or braces.

During the long wait for our turn, we could not help noticing the faces of the mothers, marked by the brand of suffering. Some seemed crushed and sat silently. Others talked and played with their children; still, the anxiety showed through.

At long last Todd's name was called, and we were ushered into a big room with many cubicles, each containing an examining table. There were several doctors working here. One was obviously elated over a little patient's improvement as she took a few halting steps toward him. The look on the mother's face was an expression of unspeakable joy.

We placed Todd on the table and took off his clothes as directed, meanwhile talking to him as if we were playing a game. All three of us were optimistic because of the marked improvement in his condition, both physical and mental, and were impatient to hear the doctor's professional opinion.

He was a handsome man, tall, straight, unsmiling, hair gray about the temples. He stood silently looking down at Todd. Then he attempted to make him sit—a wasted effort. He used his little rubber hammer on knees and elbows; Todd smiled through all this, trying to make a new friend—a wasted effort. No smile or word altered that frozen classic profile frosted with gray.

The doctor turned to face us and broke the silence by asking questions: Todd's age, his speech ability, his medical history, which none of us could supply. When he learned that I was "just" a foster mother, he addressed himself to the nurse, saying, "This is an institution case. Don't waste your time on him. Put him away." As an afterthought he added, "Write to your state representatives and tell them to stop wasting the taxpayers' money on football stadiums and build more accommodations for cases like this." And with a nod toward the small case on the table, he walked out.

I was stunned. A flip diagnosis like that, and Todd was to be tossed into the scrap bin for rejects, like a faulty casting at a foundry.

Small wonder that some grieving parent breaks under the dual burden of a handicapped child and the defective understanding of professional healers and professional comforters: "Put the child away," says the one, looking at the wall. "It's God's will," says the other, looking at the ceiling.

It occurred to me that something wonderful had happened to our family. We had taken our relationship with Todd and Robin for granted. We simply loved them; their handicap (biological defect) became almost invisible to us. They were our beautiful, happy children, entering and enjoying our family life. We placed their disabilities in rational perspective; we faced their problems in the same way we handled the learning and training problems of our own children, basically the same, yet variable for each individual child.

We sought ways to enable them to eat better; we devised diets suitable to their needs. We taught Todd— and he taught us—in a short time, means of communicating without words, with smiles or frowns, with noddings of the head in assent, or shaking it slowly in negative.

The huge advantage we had then (which we realized only later) was the absence of a mental block caused by the sorrow and shame which many parents of an exceptional child endure. When this suffering becomes too great, it completely destroys a normal relationship with the child; the result on the youngster's development can be devastating. Parents can become so absorbed in a defect that development of the normal part of the child is neglected. Frustration, self-pity, and perhaps, vegetation set in.

God knows how many great minds are sealed forever in crippled bodies for lack of simple encouragement, training, and love. How many mentally retarded, the slow-learning, able-bodied youngsters, are wasting away in institutions who could be trained to do simple tasks and contribute their bit to society, meanwhile achieving independence and fulfillment in their lives?

Until quite recently we didn't talk about an "odd" child in the family, except in tragic whispers; the child was hidden away in the home until the parents were able to place it in an institution. It was the common opinion— superstition—that such a child was divine punishment for some past sin of one parent or the other, or both of them. It was preached from the pulpit by priests who were looked upon as being privy to the mind of God.

Members of the medical profession and social agencies wrote these poor children off as monsters or vegetables with swift, terse words: "Put it away." Little wonder, then, that parents were filled with remorse, regret, fear, and horror, and that any normal relationship with such a child became paralyzed.

One reaction was complete rejection of the child; another was smothering him with a self-pitying love which crippled the child's personality (sometimes visible in the ineffable sadness in the child's eyes, sometimes in emotional outbursts of wild and vindictive actions). Again, it must be remembered, in justice, that these parents had no one to turn to for advice or encouragement.

Great strides have been taken in medical research, in education of parents, and in increased publication of articles and pamphlets by various foundations to enlighten the public. Rehabilitation centers and new schools are opening (in church basements or lodge halls—there is no room in the schools!). Still there are too many children hidden away, rejected, neglected.

We're sure that if David (the first baby), Robin, and Todd had been born of our love, our attitude toward them would have been somewhat different. However, as it was, we could receive them objectively. We chose them to enter our family, perhaps with a selfish, altruistic glow; after getting to know them, we could see the adorable little boys they were. Looking back, we feel Providence sent them to us to prepare and teach us how to love and accept our own, petite Colette.

~ 9 ~
Higher, Colette, Higher!

After months of normal activity all signs of her illness having vanished, Colette appeared to have outgrown it as the doctors had predicted. I suppose I had never really believed that Colette could be permanently ill; she was too perfect. Besides, every doctor we talked to was so vague about her phantom illness that I naturally clung to their prediction. We all settled down, indescribably happy with her recovery and with our new sons, grateful to God for this abundance of favors.

Colette loved high places and speed. In the wild, impromptu circus performances our daughters staged in the barn, Colette at the age of three would swing in a great arc on the rope high in the hayloft. At the playground she would always head for the highest sliding board; on the swings she'd beg to go higher and higher as the motion whipped her brown hair around her. She seemed transformed with the thrill of it. She always outdid her brothers on these rides. She was slim, graceful, quick, and seldom stumbled and bruised herself as her sister Sue often did while running or climbing.

Anita, Helenmarie, and Sue had bikes. Colette had always wanted one but for her safety had been denied the pleasure. Now that she seemed well, we allowed her to try riding one. Her sisters' bikes were too large for her, but she was determined and spent hours at the back steps balancing, trying to set herself and the bike in motion together.

It was during one of these practice sessions that I watched her through the back door. Suddenly there appeared that faraway, vacant expression on her face, and as her body turned, the bike slipped beneath her, and she tumbled unconscious.

How does one describe the anguish I felt? The hollow weakness as the heart is torn away? I couldn't believe that Colette had not fully recovered. She had been doing so well for so long, without a trace of trouble. We had allowed her to swim (carefully strapped in a life jacket just to be sure), to climb trees, and take hikes with her older sisters. Was all this to end for her a second time?

Again we turned to our family doctor; this time he advised us to take Colette to the Neurology Clinic at Babies' and Children's Hospital, which was part of a great medical complex. Once more she was put through endless tests and examinations; again we were given vague answers—"it resembles petit mal but it isn't." All that could be certain was that there was brain damage.

We were to hear that phrase so often: *brain damage* and *brain-damaged child*. Therefore, an article, "Theoretical Aspects of Psychological Behavior in the Brain Damaged," by Herbert Birch, Ph.D., published by the United Cerebral Palsy Association impressed me.

> Brain damage isn't a thing. There is no such thing as brain damage. There are brains which are damaged and that's an important difference. . . . And it is very doubtful that any of us here is without some damage to the brain—very doubtful. The traumata that accompany birth (I mean physical not psychoanalytic); the falls of childhood; the injuries sustained in games; the carbon monoxide poisoning that accompanies urban living; the febrile illnesses of childhood, all have left their mark on every one of us.

The doctors at the clinic encouraged us with the prospect of new drugs being developed and finding just the one for her, and it seemed as if they prescribed every one of them in the course of time. They also held out the hope (or wishful thinking) that she might outgrow it. We were warned not to permit her to go swimming, biking, or climbing; with no advance warning of her blackouts, every precaution for her safety had to be taken.

Curiously, these blackouts did not seem to worry Colette, but the restrictions on her activities did. Being singled out and left behind added to her frustration, plus the confusion from her broken train of thought. But we had no choice except to follow the doctors' orders religiously and report back to the clinic every three weeks. There were days when Colette had no blackout. I kept a daily journal in order to give the doctors accurate information.

The interdict on participation in most of the family fun chafed all of us as well as Colette; it was present in our plans for each day. It was taken for granted with Robin and Todd, because their handicap was visible; not so with Colette. She appeared perfectly normal; she was able to do everything the other children did and, at times, even better than they could; being forbidden these activities made her rebellious.

She couldn't understand, because she was not aware of having periods of unconsciousness. If she was playing with the youngsters on the floor when she passed out, she simply resumed her play on recovering consciousness. If she fell, she picked herself up and continued her play. Repeatedly we asked her if she had any strange feeling or warning of what was happening at these times. Her answer was a puzzled look. Evidently she was not in the least aware of her unconsciousness.

Every summer, about the middle of July, we had a big family picnic at an amusement park in the nearby city. There were all the latest sophisticated thrill rides, roller coasters, boat chutes, carousels, Ferris wheel. Preparing for this day was almost as much fun as the picnic itself— cookies and cakes to bake, fruit punch to mix, chicken to fry, potatoes to boil for the salad, the portable cooler to clean and cool. The excitement of the preparation days resembled the pre-Christmas spirit.

On that great day in July we were out of bed early. Anita and Helenmarie hustled getting the little ones dressed, and dishes were washed in a flash. We had a stroller for Todd, so he came along too; Robin stayed home with a baby-sitter. Todd was thrilled, enjoying the one hobby he could handle by himself—people watching. The activity, the colorful balloons and pennants (one had been tied to his chair by some friendly passerby), the shouting, running children, the booming music on the merry-go-round, the cries of the peanut and taffy vendors, and the shrieks of the passengers on the roller coasters kept an ecstatic grin on his face.

The park, tree shaded and large, was beautifully situated on the shore of Lake Erie. The amusement section is high on a bluff. There is a long, wide pier going out into the lake. Fishermen, young and old, usually line each side. There are steps leading down to it, and we were able to take Todd along and walk to the end.

We all felt as if we were on a huge ship becalmed in the middle of a sea as we looked to the blue horizon beyond which lies Canada. Todd's big smile drew people to him; he always was being invited to view a lucky fisherman's catch.

West of the amusement area was a picnic grove. Tables were spread under maples and elms, and in the center was a low-roofed pavilion, open on four sides and lined with tables. We always managed to get a big table on the north side so that we could look out over the lake, which at this time of year was an immense blue highway travelled by all manner of craft—white yachts trimmed in mahogany and brass, boats propelled by noisy outboard motors, sailboats with blinding white sails against the blue sky, and waterskiers flashing past a rowboat manned by a lone fisherman. It was a color feast for the eyes.

After the ceremony of finding a suitable table, we staked claim to it by depositing our picnic baskets, cooler, sweaters, and other impedimenta on it; then we covered everything with a tablecloth. After that there was no holding back the kids. The fresh lake breeze, seasoned with festive sounds and teasing odors, seemed to supercharge them instantly; they took off on flying legs for the nearest ride. Each had a colorful tag, tied in buttonhole or belt, entitling them to free rides on practically anything that moved in the park until sunset. This was one fringe benefit provided by Bill's company that our family enjoyed to the utmost.

Todd and Colette were left behind (small victims of short circuits in their central nervous systems); for them

the high rides and rough rides (the Whip and Dodgem)
were forbidden. We took them on a stroll to Kiddie
Land, where the amusement vehicles were reduced in
size and tempo; there we had rides on the Merry-go-
ride, pony carts, and Sleepy Hollow R.R., a little train
that travelled through a sylvan park over small bridges,
past a red mill's pond with golden carp swimming under
water lily pads, and a miniature village. After three rides
on this, even the golden carp lost their glow; two little
heads kept turning toward the park area where the action was, from which came ecstatic screams and the
sounds of the cars on the roller coasters.

Colette decided to appeal to her mother's competitive
spirit, "Mommy, why can't I go on the racing coasters?
Anita will take me if you're afraid to go on." We tried to
change the subject by pointing with artificial vivacity to
another slow and low ride. But the ponies seemed to be
getting dead tired; the Merry-go-ride had palled. That
and Colette's longing and pleading were too much for
us. "I don't see why I can't take her on some of the high
rides if I hang on to her," I said. Bill said, "Todd and I
will watch you." Todd nodded vigorous assent.

We started with the Whip; she weathered it fine, no
fear, no blackout, and Colette wanted more. Then we
tried a medium high ride; she hung on to me and I
wrapped one arm around her and clung to the seat bar
with the other. Before long we were taking the high
rides like old pros; she screamed with the thrill of the
breathtaking descent, her eyes ablaze, her pigtails flying
out behind her. Below, Todd watched, enjoying it all,
almost as much as we did.

Colette would have gone on endlessly except for one
thing—I couldn't take it. But she was content to sit on a
bench and talk on and on to Todd and dad about her
indescribable fun.

After an action-filled day, with few scraps of food left
in our picnic basket, we piled our gear and our family
into the car and headed for home. Helenmarie, Sue,
Eric, and David were comparing notes in the back seat:
how many rides each one had on this, how many on
that. It all seemed unbelievable but wonderfully true.
Before we were halfway home a quiet descended upon

us, the little ones drifting into sleep, the older ones watching familiar scenes go by, or dreaming of the future.

My own happiest silent memory was that Colette had the same fun the rest had had; there had been a risk, but wasn't there a risk for everyone who stepped into one of those flying cars? As long as she was small and our arms (and stomachs) were strong enough, she was going to have that fun.

After that experience we decided to let Colette go back to swimming. Bill extended a rope between two trees close to the bank; here she could paddle about in a life jacket, and we were nearby to watch her in case she lost consciousness.

It wasn't that our child's safety no longer concerned us; on the contrary, we watched her constantly without its being too obvious to her. She was never without someone close by to catch her falling body, but we were convinced that it was just as important that she share in normal play. The psychic hazards of a lost childhood were, in our minds, more real, immediate, and terrible than muscular bumps, bruises, or fractures.

And so we gave her back the bike.

～ 10 ～
The Redhead

It was the end of June. Colette and I had an appointment for a triweekly checkup. As we walked from the parking lot to the hospital, her steps faltered; that faraway look spread over her face, and she slid into unconsciousness. I knelt beside her, shading her from the blazing sun, waiting for her to regain consciousness. I didn't need a clinic to tell me she wasn't improving; these blackouts continued, and no amount or combination of medication helped.

The doctor listened to my recital of her day-by-day record since our last visit, put Colette through what was becoming a routine examination of the eyes, and tapped her knees and elbows with his little rubber hammer, meanwhile making notes. Over and over again, I was asked to describe what happened when her spells occurred. Once more we were told that she was an unusual case and were given a dose of verbal assurance that she could be helped. A new prescription was handed to me, and another episode of futility ended.

Colette did not mind these visits; she enjoyed meeting the doctors and nurses. The long drive was always an adventure for her; sometimes we stopped for lunch or visited a friend. In warm weather we would stop at a drive-in which served an endless menu of cool combinations of ice cream and carbonated drinks, over which she pondered for, seemingly, endless minutes before making the big decision.

On this oppressively warm afternoon, returning from another frustrating visit with the doctors, my spirits were lowered by the discomfort of driving in heavy traffic in a glaring sun, and I found myself succumbing to self-pity. Why did this have to happen to us (me); why, God? If our child had to be handicapped, why could it not be something visible and easily diagnosed, something with which we could cope or accept?

The veiled nature of Colette's malaise was what seemed unbearable. I rebelled against Providence (paradox?) almost wishing Colette were like Robin or Todd; in short, demanding the right to choose a cross to fit my preference. I was infected with a self-pity which, if allowed to grow, can destroy a person; I felt it burning within me, smothering hope, love, and laughter.

Colette was quiet as she sat next to me; she sensed my sadness. It was too warm even to sing, as we often did on these long drives, belting "Que Sera" or "Frere Jacques." Perspiration dampened her forehead, and little drops curled the loose strands of hair at her temples. Her long braids seemed to wilt over her shoulders.

"Look, kitten," I said, "as soon as we get home you can slip into your bathing suit and go for a nice cool swim." This promise seemed to perk up her drooping spirit. As we rounded the last turn and saw the gray slate roof among the tall trees, it seemed like a cool oasis. Colette barely waited for the car to stop before she hopped out and raced to the house to change; I had to shout to remind her to bring her life jacket.

Except Anita, who was baby-sitting in the house, the rest of the children were splashing and swimming in the lake. When Helenmarie heard she was arriving, she came running, glistening and dripping water all the way. "There was a phone call just after you left, mom. The woman didn't say who she was, but she gave me a phone number and said it was urgent." Her message delivered, she took off and dove into the water with a splash.

The call was from Child Welfare. "We have a desperate case here and we wondered if you would help us. We have a three-year-old girl who must be placed immediately; she is a hydrocephalic and retarded child, but she is no problem to feed or care for, as Robin is. She can't walk, but possibly some day she will."

The request startled me; it was like cold water splashed in my face, rousing me from a terrible nightmare; I was

confused and disoriented. I replied that I couldn't give
her an answer immediately but would call her in the
morning.

As I replaced the receiver, a feeling of shame spread
over me. The Spanish proverb, I complained because I
had no shoes until I met a man who had no feet, kept
ringing in my mind. Colette, who had been standing
beside me in her swimsuit, handed me her life jacket,
and as I tied the bright orange vest on her, I kept
repeating silently, "There is no time for tears."

I walked out with her and settled in a lawn chair under
a tall cottonwood tree to watch her. The water is cold
since the pond is spring fed, and Colette gingerly put
one foot in, then jerked it out. After a few such tests,
she grabbed the rope Bill had placed between two trees
and plunged in. She spread out her slim body and pretended she was swimming, kicking her feet while holding on to the rope; she looked so normal, so perfect.

The others continued their ball game in the water,
shrieking and teasing one another. Somehow, when kids
get into water they sound noisier. As I sat there I thought
of the little girl who desperately lacked a home; I didn't
even know her name. I was overcome with a wave of
sadness—the heartbreak in life. At the same moment
came the realization, the counterpoint, that I could as-
suage a wee part of the heartbreak by opening my arms
to this child.

I emerged from my smothering sadness; it was as
though a cool breeze had sprung up and swept away the
oppressive heat. There was no doubt in my mind this
time; we had to take this little girl, at least temporarily,
until something could be worked out for her. What was
one more? We had the room, and we had learned much
these past few years caring for Robin and Todd.

That evening, as we were gathered at the dinner table,
I told the family about the little orphan. I used a more
positive approach this time, "I think we should take her
at least temporarily, don't you think so?" Bill and the
others nodded vigorous approval. Again the household
took on the excitement of anticipation; only this time
Todd joined in it; he squealed in delight.

Ethel arrived the next afternoon. She lay rigid on the

back seat of the social worker's car. She seemed afraid to move a muscle. I carried her into the house and placed her in the crib the girls had brought from the attic.

Her head wasn't too large and didn't seem out of proportion to her body, which was large and chubby for her age—so unlike little David, our first foster son. She didn't look hydrocephalic.

She had auburn red hair and fair skin; her eyes were violet blue. She was a thoroughly frightened child and uttered a lusty howl as I placed her in the crib. She held herself rigid, not moving her head one way or the other, fearful of shattering the fragile shell she had wished around herself to hide in.

Despite her fright, she was a beautiful child.

The social worker had little to offer in the way of instructions; I was on my own. She left a small paper bag holding the child's clothing. I thanked her and after a polite good-bye, returned to the bedroom.

All seven children were there, surrounding the crib, trying to pacify the occupant, who was upholding the tradition of the temperament of redheads. She had a temper, and she was mad, letting the world know she didn't like change of any kind. But before long her bed was piled with toys, her tears disappeared, and she was wreathed in smiles. Wonder of wonders, she spoke two words, "Hi, Cookie," over and over again.

At dinner that evening Susie seemed to have something on her mind; she was unusually quiet. Finally, the thought surfaced. "The name Ethel," she said, "doesn't seem to fit our family."

"But we can't change her name."

"Why not?"

"Her parents gave her that name, and it must have special meaning to them."

"Well," Eric interposed, "some of us have nicknames: Anita is Tidi, Helenmarie is Tommie, Suzanne is Suzie, Colette is Chichi. Why can't we give her a nickname?"

That seemed reasonable enough. We asked if they had any name in mind.

"I think," said Helenmarie, judiciously, "with her

red hair and hot temper she must have some Irish in her, so I think we ought to call her Kelly.''

Approval was unanimous, and from that day the name Ethel was heard no more in our midst. But Kelly, with a grand simplicity, addressed everyone, large or small, friend or stranger, doctor or priest, ''Hi, Cookie!''

~11~
The Terrible Tearer

Kelly had boundless vitality, a zest for fun and boisterous play. She had a deep, hearty laugh to express full approval, a silly little giggle for moderate appreciation, and a full-bodied, house-vibrating howl to express dissent. A simple mechanical toy or a brightly colored ball would send her into an ecstasy of laughter, her blue eyes sparkling, red curls bouncing.

For the first few weeks, Kelly seemed only to want to be left in bed; there her rigid legs kicked so vigorously that the bed shook and slowly moved across the room. If we placed her on the floor or in the play pen, she would send up howls of disapproval, the protests of a little bird that did not want to leave its nest. We also tried taking her outdoors, stretching her out flat in Todd's stroller with its little protective canopy, but again she shrieked her disapproval. Or was it discomfort? We didn't know.

Although she could be the noisiest member of the household, Kelly went into frenzied crying jags when there was a sudden loud noise, such as the sound of a truck exhaust or a power lawn mower outside her window. Even as she grew older and was able to sit in her wheelchair outdoors, she could not be left there when the children were swimming. Their cries and laughter struck painful vibrations for her, and she screamed with pain and terror.

Gradually, as the weeks passed, she came to trust us and allowed us to take her out of her bed. The next step was the playpen, which we set up in the corner of the kitchen. Here she joined Todd as spectator of the rites of cooking, baking, eating.

She began to develop a strong pitching arm. Any toy we might give her soon came sailing across the kitchen followed by peals of laughter. We soon learned to separate wood blocks and metal cars from rubber balls, stuffed dolls, and animals. We never could quite figure out what delighted her more—the hurling, or a target hit.

The next step was to get her to sit. We tried the Teeterbabe, but it was too small and flopped over on the first try, sending her into tears. A friend gave us an old wooden highchair, the kind that collapsed and could be converted into a low chair with a play table in front. This gave it a broad base to prevent tipping over.

We tucked Kelly in with pillows, and gradually, with a little practice each day, she learned to sit. She loved it and would play for hours in her funny brown chair. We'd place a box of toys beside her; she'd take them out one by one and maybe play with one on her little table or throw them all about the room.

We discovered she fancied the bright colors of old greeting cards. She could be content with one card, turning it about, enjoying the colors, chuckling to herself; or she could go through a dozen, tearing them to bits, flinging them into the air, and watching her homemade confetti sprinkling down about her. There was always a cleanup job after Kelly's play sessions.

Each foster child is provided with medical needs and clothing. When one is in need of new items, a request is placed with the social worker. Since Kelly came almost empty-handed, we were sent a purchase order to buy clothes for her at a nearby department store.

Sue and Helenmarie accompanied me on a shopping trip. We went in the evening, when the little ones were bedded down. Our shopping list included underwear, playsuits, dresses, and sleepers. The girls reminded me of veteran shoppers the way they went through the piles and racks of clothing, searching for just the right colors and sizes, always with an eye for the most attractive style for Kelly.

As they selected things, I checked them for serviceability and price; there was a definite limit on the latter.

When the wardrobe was complete, we gathered our bundles and headed for home. Sue and Helenmarie were excited about their choices and eager to see how the colorful and gay garments would look on their little foster sister.

After breakfast next morning, Sue volunteered to feed and dress Kelly. I could visualize her going through the neat piles of new clothes in Kelly's bureau drawer, deciding just the right one for her little charge. Later, as I bathed Robin, Sue came in and exclaimed, "Oh, mom! She's so cute. She seems to be quite taken with her new outfit; go in and take a look at her."

"In a minute, Sue. I have to finish Robin first."

Sue took off to find Helenmarie.

With the last dab at putting Robin's room in order after the bath, I remembered Kelly and crossed the hall to get a glimpse of the first showing of her new wardrobe. I stopped in my tracks as I entered her room. I stared in disbelief at our curly-headed beauty. She was half naked—the upper half. How could she do it? As I stood there in a state of shock, that beautiful little doll chirped, "Hi, Cookie," as she tossed a button towards me. On the bed and all over the floor lay her playsuit, torn in a hundred bits. She picked up a piece and tore it while I watched. She was having the time of her life.

Sue and her sisters came in, and after one glance gave off agonizing teenage shrieks. These being above Kelly's noise threshold, she in turn shrieked, surpassing them all.

"Good grief, how will we ever keep her in clothes?"

We began trying to solve the problem by going through her clothing and removing nonessentials: the decorative buttons, clasps, ribbons, and dress ties. We had discovered on close examination of the ruined suit that she apparently started this tearing spree by ripping off a colorful button.

We made certain that she had a good supply of toys and cards after she was dressed. This seemed to solve the problem for the moment; she would go for days without noticing her clothing.

It was but a lull; one after the other these outfits were reduced to shreds; she was, it seems, a periodic nudist.

It became a sort of wait and watch game for Kelly's Doukhobor urges.

I became a regular customer at rummage sales and a used clothing store in a neighboring town, picking up dresses and playsuits for a few cents. Friends rallied to the cause and sent garments their children had outgrown.

All of this, however, did not solve the problem. After experimenting with sleeping bags, trundle bundles, and the like, we designed a type of gown for Kelly which was devoid of trimmings, buttons, collars, cuffs, or loose ends. These looked like straight nightgowns, but the bottoms were sewed shut.

Kelly couldn't pull these gowns up to get them off, nor could she get at the hem to begin her tearing process. They were fastened up the back with a long zipper which she couldn't reach, and all the seams were reinforced. Kelly looked like the comic-strip character Peewee, scooting around the floor with her long gown trailing behind her. Whatever the gown lacked in frills and furbelows was compensated for in vibrant colors and gay prints; her wardrobe now contained a stack of rainbow-colored gowns. And when these wore out from normal wear (and not tear) they were replaced with others of the same style and material.

Kelly had a thing about eating also. She wouldn't put food in her mouth; it was more fun to play with it. Over and over we tried to teach her to feed herself, but for her the food was just something to dabble in. She would eat heartily enough if one fed her, but left to herself, she splashed the contents of her bowl about, finger painting any available surface with artistic abandon. The result was as messy as most modern art.

In addition to her ability to unravel the tightest weave of the toughest textiles, she possessed an internal motive power to propel any stationary object she was placed in. Secured in her wheelchair, which had a brake on each wheel, plus a fifty-pound building block strapped behind it as an anchor, she could propel herself across twenty feet of space in a matter of ten minutes. She began to develop this talent for locomotion (own prime mover) at about age five. She shuffled about in her bed, usually to a window, where she worked havoc on the venetian blind.

At first, this seemed a simple problem to solve; we removed the castors from the bed. Kelly gleefully accepted this in true competitive spirit; she soon moved the bed around without the castors. Her gay greeting, "Hi, Cookie," we interpreted as "Look, mom, no hands!" (or more appropriately, no castors).

Our next move in this game was to screw hooks on the baseboard and matching eyes on the two inner legs of the bed; thus fastening the bed to the wall. Checkmate! She took this in sportsmanlike fashion—one game does not make a season—and began to practice her true metier by ripping sheets and mattress cover to enjoy the soft feel of mattress batting as she tore it apart.

～ 12 ～
The Winter Additions

At this time we had room for two more children and help to care for them; so Michael and Johnny joined our family.

Michael arrived in the middle of winter; he was a microcephalic child. He had been cared for by his mother and grandmother, but in a car-truck collision his grandmother was killed and his mother critically injured.

The thing that seemed so remarkable to us about Michael was that he could walk. We had grown accustomed to the confinement to bed or chair of the other three foster children. There were shouts, "Look, he walks," from the children when they first saw him. His ability to ambulate seemed miraculous (indeed it was when one pauses to think of it—one of the minute miracles which, taken together, make up that piece of work, a human being).

Michael was six years old, and like Todd, he had a twin sister who was perfectly normal. He was extremely tiny; he wore size-two clothing, but did not have the chubby, baby features of a two-year-old. On the contrary, he had features that made him seem old and knowledgeable—a diminutive dark Irishman with tight black curls and deep elfish eyes, that looked on the world with an amused squint. He made a convincing model, if one were needed to sketch a leprechaun.

Thinking back, it seems strange that none of us ever called him Mike; it was always Michael, perhaps in subconscious respect for his otherworldly dignity.

He was a quiet child; keeping to himself, he seldom

laughed or cried; it is hard to realize that he died of violence; but that was years later in a state school.

He had delicate features and a milk white skin. His blue eyes were strangely beautiful; strange because they never focused on you. He seemed always to be looking intently at some mysterious far-off place or object; we never felt as if we had eye contact with him.

His hands and feet were so small as to be almost birdlike. He had a custom of cupping and turning his hands near his eyes, examining and enjoying whatever he saw. The kaleidoscopic designs he made with them fascinated him. He enjoyed his hands more than any toy we could give him, although he always wanted his wooden soldier and a small, red dime-store tractor close by. These too, he held off at various angles for viewing. He was entranced it seemed by the shadows or shapes they took on instead of the toys themselves; he never made the tractor work or run on its wheels as it was intended to do. He didn't seem to know what it was nor to care to know.

He was extremely active—hyperactive—reminding one of a hummingbird with his tiny birdlike features and perpetual motion. He darted from one place to another, seeming to settle down only to swirl around and head in another direction in continuous animation. His activity was exhausting to watch and, indeed, it must have been so for him for finally he would come to rest in a big chair or on the floor to continue his hand play, until he dropped off into a nap. He slept as exhausted as a little boy lost.

The pleasing novelty of having this small boy darting about the house wore off quickly; we realized that we couldn't keep up with his activity; there were the safety hazards to consider. He didn't seem to watch or care where he was heading: as a consequence, lamps were overturned, end tables upended, forts and whole cities destroyed (as the archangel Michael may destroy the cities on the last day). Michael trampling was accompanied by wails of anguish from Todd and David. Michael himself seemed unhappy with the obstructions and creatures on the floor hindering his freedom of movement.

There was a spare room at the back of the house which had been a waiting room for patients in the days of the doctor. It was small, as is customary with doctors' waiting rooms, and it adjoined a much larger room (formerly the doctor's office), which we used as a study and later as another bedroom. This small room, bright with light from its one window, seemed to be waiting for Michael.

We bought a folding gate and installed it in the doorway; he could see and hear us, although confined. Michael solved the problem of the gate almost immediately by climbing over it, pleasing us by this show of intelligence and initiative. We called the lumber company and ordered a sheet of fiber board, which we cut in half. We fastened one piece to the gate, thus making a sort of dutch door; and since Michael couldn't see through it, he had to be satisfied with merely hearing us. He took it philosophically and settled down in his winter playroom undisturbed by the other children, free to move about as he chose.

There was security for him in this private play area, and he was happy in his uncluttered haven. We discovered he did not like toys and furniture about him, save his tiny tractor and wooden soldier.

Girls especially he didn't want around him, cluttering up his wee universe. One time we thought it might be fun for Kelly (the strip artist) to join Michael in his playroom. She had learned to scoot around on the floor hinderwise (in a sitting postion).

Her visit turned into a traumatic nightmare for Michael; for Kelly it was like the good old times. Somehow she cornered her playmate and undressed him; when we came running in response to Michael's cry of protest, we found him standing bare and frightened, and Kelly sitting there with a heap of clothing beside her, which blissfully she was beginning to tear. After that, Michael was left alone to dart quietly about, to hum and rehearse his finger operas, or to drop into a renewing nap.

Michael brought with him, among his personal clothing, a sleeping jacket of unusual design. It was made of heavy muslin, sleeveless and tied down the back: really it was a long vest with long, strong tie-cords (three on each side) which one secured to the bedspring or bottom bar of the bed. This jacket proved to be a necessary sleeping garment for him and later for other active children we had; without it Michael would have been out of his bed in a flash and roaming about the house on his sleepless nights (usually when the moon was full). The jacket allowed freedom of arms and legs and limited movement of the rest of the body but prevented the child from standing or climbing over the bed rail.

Usually, at first, a child fiercely resists the jacket, but soon he comes to depend on it as a source of comfort and security, much like an old blanket or a favorite teddy bear which some children adopt for sleeping companions.

There were nights when one could hear Michael humming or laughing to himself, communing with angels or leprechauns perhaps, his tiny hands constantly gyrating in arabesques.

We noted over the years that when the moon was full, Michael was especially keyed up, sleepless, and hyperactive. He would go for several days without sleep and then sink, exhausted and weeping, into profound slumber. At such times he would curl up in some convenient lap and, clinging tight, absorb all the comfort and love one could pour on him. At other times he rejected personal contact with anyone.

He could not feed himself; his fluttering hands refused the spoon. We held his hands down, and this slight restraint seemed a source of comfort and relief to him, similar to the restraint of the bed jacket at night. His compulsive activity restrained, he could enjoy his food; chocolate cake he liked especially, and ice cream.

Baby John arrived the following October. He was an orphan. He was with us only a few months; but they were months of agonizing pain for him, compassionate agony for us. He had an incurable brain tumor which sent pain surging through his frail body, grotesquely twisting his thin face. His only relief was the blessed oblivion that followed taking his prescribed pain-killing and sleep-inducing medication.

For us it was a daily suffering to stand by and watch this forlorn waif, unable to help him, listening to his despairing wails. The normally analgesic rhythm of the rocking chair had no effect on John; pain was a parasite feeding on his whole being with ten thousand needle-sharp teeth. During long night hours, we would walk the floor with him, although he gave no sign that it helped in the least. Perhaps we did it in a vain effort to share his burden of intolerable woe; perhaps it was merely a way to weariness, to bring us sleep.

Unspoken questions raced through the mind during this walking in the night hours: why the incurable suffering of an innocent child? That is the way it was with Johnny: we rocked him; we walked him; we wept with him and stormed heaven with prayers for a quick merciful release from this excruciating, hopeless pain. He was with us a few months—they seemed long years.

All the rooms of the house (fourteen) were now filled; Robin and Johnnie shared one bedroom, Todd, Kelly, and Michael shared another. The five bedrooms upstairs were occupied by Gauchats, young and old, plus all the paraphernalia girls and boys gather and treasure (forever, it seems).

Our daily household routine took a new order; meals were scheduled for the little ones to avoid overlapping with our family meals, especially the evening meal which has always been one of lively discussions, varying with ages and interests. Todd was the only one who joined us at the table and was an active auditor in the discussions, his expressive features registering approval or a vigorous veto to opinions expressed.

Baths were staggered during the day for the young children, leaving a tub available in the evening for the older ones; a tight laundry schedule had to be maintained: washing, drying, folding, sorting. Careful planning produced an unhurried routine that was pleasant for everyone.

When Mike wasn't in his playroom, Kelly could enjoy it, scooting around the waxed linoleum floor. Todd had been enrolled at a nearby therapy center, and went twice a week for treatments.

Except for David, all of our children were in school, and it wasn't until the last of them were school-bound that the little ones started their day.

September gales stripped the trees, and heavy snow in October forecast a long cold winter; but indoors all seemed snug and comfortable. A routine had been established, and we took pride in how smoothly our large household was functioning. It was a daily joy to watch each child develop and find his measure of happiness—save for Johnnie, whose suffering increased as the nights lengthened.

The winter was not only long and severe, with continued snow storms and a brief interval of floods in January, but also it was one of prolonged and serious illness.

~ 13 ~
Death Defeated

Perhaps the brilliant morning sunlight on the fresh snow, making all familiar things new, was the reason I did not feel the vague foreboding usually experienced when I approached the classic facade of the hospital. My step felt firm and light; my spirit buoyant, happy; I had come to take Robin home. He had been hospitalized for a week with one of his frightening respiratory infections but was now well again and ready for release. Oxygen and antibiotics had produced another victory for him.

With the pink release slip in one hand and a bundle of his clothing in the other, I strode into his room, eager to get him dressed and home. I handed the release to the nurse, who was working on Robin's roommate, on the other side of the glass partition separating the beds.

I proceeded to dress Robin. His broad smile told me he recognized me, and I felt he knew he was going home. He looked well.

As I was finishing dressing him, I noticed the nurse pushing the crib of her small patient from its cubicle.

"Moving out?" I inquired.

"She's developed a rash. We're moving her to a private room, just to make sure."

"But what about Robin?" I was unable to ask her that question. I put it aside, thinking the doctor surely must have taken steps to protect Robin.

In the lobby I covered Robin's face with the blanket I had wrapped him in and snuggled him close to me as I pushed the door open, leaving in a gust of cold air. The frigid air pinched my nostrils and made my breath visible before me. The bright sun on the snow created an illusion of warmth that the bitter cold dispelled.

At home all was quiet, even Johnnie, who slept deeply after his morning dose of medicine. Gert and Catherine, our invaluable aides, welcomed Robin, our little bird, home.

The house was clean and orderly after the magic touch of Gert's hard-working hands. The children, washed and dressed, were playing.

Robin sensed his home; sounds and smells to the sightless are the avenues to recognition and memory, as familiar faces and places are to us who have the gift of seeing. He knew he was in his own bed and recognized the melody emanating from the music box in the belly of his panda bear, sitting in a corner of the crib. Drawing a deep breath, Robin sniffed the soft sheet beneath him and sighed contentedly—secure in his own nest.

We ate lunch and were just finishing coffee when the doorbell rang, startling Kelly into frenzied howling. This stirred Johnnie into anguished consciousness and cries of pain; in a sudden chain reaction, the house was rocked with activity, noise, and tears.

Our visitor, when she entered, seemed awed by the noise and upheaval caused by the tip of her forefinger on a small bell-button and somewhat embarrassed for calling at an inopportune time. Her name was Anna. She was a small, shy woman, always dressed in black; she had no relatives in this country and was lonely. She had heard about the children and came occasionally to visit, bringing candy and toys.

Gert took her coat while I assured her things weren't as bad as they sounded. She stopped by Todd's standing-table and patted his head and talked to him; he gave his widest smile and enthusiastic nods of his head in welcome. I was about to put Johnnie back in his crib, for it was time to prepare the children's lunch. She spread her arms, asking whether she might hold him and rock him. Gratefully I handed Johnnie to her. She settled down in the rocking chair beside his bed, speaking softly to him.

In the kitchen I set up the children's trays as Catherine washed hands and put on bibs. I wanted to feed Johnnie first, hoping it would help soothe away his tears;

he was on a special diet of goat's milk and selected fruits and vegetables, being allergic to many foods. At this period, the medical opinion was that his pain, vomiting, and frequent high temperatures were caused by allergies (allergy was fashionable at the time).

Johnnie's solid food was blended with his milk in the highspeed blender and fed to him in a bottle with an enlarged nipple—the way we fed Robin. After I had given him his medication, Anna offered to feed Johnnie; so I rejoined Catherine in the kitchen, and we began the noon ritual of feeding Kelly, Mike, and Todd.

The last notes of querulous weeping faded away in the clinking of spoons and the satisfied sighs of our diners. We could hear Anna moving about in the next room crooning to Johnnie; she had a special love for him, always singling him out when she visited. He was quiet now; for a while chronic pain and hunger pangs were submerged.

"I changed him and put him back to bed," Anna told me as she came into the kitchen with her coat over her arm. "He seemed drowsy, maybe he'll sleep," she said as she slipped into her coat.

Her next words to me were fearfully disconcerting. "Sorry, I can't stay longer, but I have the darndest sore throat. I'd better get home and doctor it."

I closed the door in a fury of foreboding. How thoughtless can an adult person be—visiting a sick child while probably carrying a host of *streptococci* in her throat! She didn't realize how vulnerable children are to every infection. Impatiently I tried to brush away my feeling of fear, "Don't press the panic button; besides there's nothing you can do now," I said aloud.

The weather continued cold, to the delight of our children; the snow was deep and the lake frozen solid. After invigorating hours of shovelling and scraping the pond, they had cleared a large circular area for skating. Now every afternoon after school our natural ice rink swirled with gay, colorful, noisy skaters, and Todd was out there among them. Looking out the window, I watched one of the neighbor boys carefully pulling Todd's sled as if it contained some fragile object.

Todd resented this kid glove treatment. He frowned

and wriggled his displeasure. I could see Eric gliding toward them. He took the rope of the sled, dug in with his skates, and raced across the ice, cutting sharp corners and causing the sled to skid and slew in wide semicircles.

I could see that our visitor was concerned about Todd, but Todd shouted with delight. We must always keep remembering that an exceptional child is always more normal than abnormal; just as we should remember that a person who speaks broken English does not also suffer from impaired hearing.

Robin developed symptoms of a cold a week after I had brought him home from the hospital; a few days more and he was sniffling and coughing and had a high temperature. Todd and Johnnie were gripped with attacks of vomiting, and a raging fever sapped their strength, leaving them lethargic and pitifully sick. Todd pointed to his throat and nodded when I asked if it hurt.

With Johnnie the symptoms were not unusual, frequently he vomited (the allergies), and a high temperature for him was usual, not unusual (the effects of the brain tumor). But with Todd, sickness was rare; despite his frail frame, he had been a healthy child since he joined our family. He was very ill now.

I set about giving each of the ailing ones aspirin and an alcohol bath to reduce the fever. All three refused to eat; except for an occasional wail from Johnnie and a cough from Robin, they lay ominously quiet. There are times when a mother knows without study, reflection, or reason that grave danger threatens her child. This was such a time.

I called the doctor and asked him to come as soon as he could. He said it would probably be evening before he could call. I stifled a surge of irritation by recalling that the few doctors in our county worked long hours. I paged through my worn copy of a baby care book. As I read, I grew sure that what Todd had was scarlet fever.

Late that evening, the doctor arrived, looking exhausted. After a silent examination of the sick trio, he gave me the grim news—professional confirmation of the afternoon's black thoughts: Todd and Johnnie had scarlet fever; Robin had measles.

The doctor jotted down prescriptions for each of the patients and for the healthy members of the household. "All of you will have to take antibiotics as a protection against scarlet fever. Keep the children out and away from the rooms of the sick ones. Every time you go in, wear a smock and mask and scrub your hands thoroughly after caring for them."

I was gripped alternately by two waves of fear—fear for the life of the sick (I had been told that measles invariably were fatal to a child who suffered a handicap such as Robin's) and also for the safety of our own brood.

Bill left immediately for the drug store, stuffing the prescriptions into his pocket.

Through the next three weeks, the nights were broken into naps, nursing chores, and nightmares. Todd was scarlet from head to toes. His lips were parched. He craved cold water, even though it meant a struggle to swallow each drop.

The other patients, Robin and Johnnie, refused all fluids; comatose, they seemed unaware of what was going on around them. Death, silent, seemed imminent. The doctor must have felt this too; though he said nothing. After several days of burning fevers and no fluid intake, the two would have to be given fluid through the tissues— "clysis, it's called," the doctor told me offhandedly.

"This means the hospital for them," I said.

Wearily he shook his head. "I'll bring you a supply of glucose and hypodermic needles, and show you how it's done. They must have fluids—you'll inject them in the morning and evening."

"But I don't think I can," I protested.

"I'll teach you." With that he left to get the supplies.

Gritting my teeth, I repeated to myself, "I can't do it; I won't do it." But by the time the doctor returned, I was confident that I could and would do it. I had two burning desires—to keep these children alive and to protect my children from harm.

Bill and I held a brainstorming session on ways and means to keep the contagion confined. We divided the house. The sick wing (the isolation ward) was off limits for everyone, including Catherine—the poor girl was gripped with fear that she would contract the fever or bring it home to her younger brothers and sisters. Only I entered the sick rooms.

Thanks to frozen foods and the budding domestic skills of Anita, our eldest, meals were prepared and lunches packed. The children sensed, without fully understanding, the gravity of the crisis and rallied to the cause, pitching in with household chores and cooperating with one another in a way I'll probably never see again.

Both arms burdened, the doctor returned with boxes of bottled glucose, plastic tubes, and hypodermic needles. From wire coat hangers, he fashioned hooks to hold the bottles of fluid; these he hung from the window latch. We drew the beds closely together.

After boiling the needles, he showed me how to inject one under the skin on Robin's back, being careful first to wipe the area with alcohol and then check the tubing for air bubbles. It seemed quite simple when the doctor's hands did it. I watched him as he adjusted the clamp to regulate the flow and rehearsed in my mind each step: sterilize needle, insert needle in tubing, wipe skin with alcohol, check for air bubbles, inject needle just under the skin, check flow, watch that it goes in properly—otherwise the fluid would collect in one area causing it to bulge out painfully and the needle would have to be inserted in another area. "Now, you do Johnnie," the doctor said, turning to me. I had been in a trance of concentration watching him handle Robin and memorizing the procedure. Now I was petrified with fright—stage fright: dry mouth, clammy hands, funny tummy, weak knees, irresponsible wishes. (Why hadn't I become a nurse instead of wasting my youth studying art?)

My hands trembled as I tried to insert a needle into the plastic tube. I felt the same as when I gave David (the first David, hydrocephalic with spina bifida) his first bath, and as then, I prayed, "Dear God, help me— steady my hands."

My faith confirmed, my hands steadied; I followed each step, and finally, swiftly and surely, inserted the needle between skin and muscle. It worked, proving to me it was all part of a miracle.

Slowly the precious fluid dripped into the dehydrated bodies. For five days, two times a day, I continued the tube feeding. However, there was no perceptible improvement; Robin and Johnnie seemed to be hanging on to life by a thread. Todd, after ten days, contracted measles, and his condition worsened.

The next morning Catherine, our girl Friday, who in the course of a few months—despite a language and culture gap—had become a member of the family, packed her cardboard suitcase and left.

"I'm scared," she told me.

I could not be angry with her; who could blame her for not wanting to risk her health? Loyalty and heroism cannot be had for hire—they are spontaneous gifts, unexpected, unusual.

I felt desperately alone, exhausted from my nursing chores, every nerve screaming the need for sleep, overwhelmed with the responsibility that forced me to think, to grope for the right answers, here and now, to two problems: Todd's turn for the worse, and the lack of help for the coming day. I would be forced to leave the contagious area to care for the healthy youngsters; perhaps infect them.

First things first—to get help for Todd, whose temperature kept on rising to 106° despite bathing and ice packs. Blearily I dialed the home number of the doctor, fearful of waking him from sleep and fearful also that he might have started on his rounds. When I heard his voice I begged him to come quickly. Coldly polite, he said, "Impossible." He would be tied up with patients all day long. But Todd was a patient of his, and Robin and Johnnie—had he given up on them?

"Impossible!" he said.

I sat staring at the phone, crushed. Did the doctor's "impossible", translated from polite code, mean: "Why should I inconvenience respectable patients, pillars of the community, for nameless wards of the county, waifs. I ask you is that reasonable?"

Impossible!

Staring at the cradled phone, I realized that subconsciously I was resigned and awaiting fearfully the coming of death for Robin and Johnnie; their chance of living had been slight even before this latest illness struck. But not Todd—Todd was always such a vital little tiger, fighting against impossible odds from the day he was born. I could not stop fighting alongside him now.

It was hopeless without immediate medical care. To whom could I turn? Then it clicked, and I reached for the phone. Todd's father! If my mind had not been drugged with exhaustion, it would have occurred immediately. Almost daily I had kept him abreast of Todd's condition; but not early in the morning, of course. Thank God, he had not left for work, and I explained Todd's latest complication and the great urgency of getting a doctor.

"I'll be there within the hour, and I'll have an M.D. with me," he said quickly, confidently.

My tone must have sounded dubious. "How can you be sure?"

"Because this doctor is a friend of mine. We went to school together. He is getting an office in order to begin his practice here."

Soon afterward the doctor arrived. His quick understanding and unhurried manner of examining the children, questioning me on the history of each one, lifted from me the weight of helplessness.

He was candid; there was little he could do. We had to get Todd's fever down and keep it down; if there was no improvement by next morning, Todd would have to be taken to Metropolitan Hospital, which had a wing for contagious diseases—the same place we had taken Colette when she was stricken by encephalitis during her bout with whooping cough.

The night passed in prayerful watchfulness at Todd's bed. We dropped water into his mouth with an eyedropper; his room was fogged with steam in an endeavor to saturate him with moisture, but little was absorbed into his desiccated body. The raging fever was a demon possessing his body, to be driven out by prayer and water.

By morning the fever was down; the doctor arrived early and was satisfied there was enough improvement to postpone any transfer to the hospital. This slight encouragement raised our spirits. We thanked him and told him we had a question.

During our long nocturnal vigil, Bill and I had discussed our past difficulties in getting care. Perhaps, now, this doctor, a friend of Todd's father, might be willing to take care of all the children. He was young, seemed dedicated, and appeared genuinely interested in our damaged youngsters. As human beings, they had an equal right to medical service. Unfortunately (as experience had taught us) their needs often are brushed aside on the excuse that they are hopeless cases, and professional time and resources should be allotted to the normal individuals. This is nothing less than acceptance of survival of the fittest—a principle enthusiastically espoused by the merciless Hitler and his Nazis.

Our question to the doctor was, "Will you be our family physician—family to include all our foster children, present and future?"

He said, "Surely, provided you notify your present physician that this is what you want. Medical ethics," he added with a smile. Maybe he said, "Professional ethics," but anyway that was the gist of it.

Our former doctor sounded relieved when we informed him of our decision. It was a hard winter on doctors everywhere that year.

As the days passed there appeared some slight improvement in Robin and Todd; while their temperatures lingered several degrees above normal, they began to take nourishment and give signs of interest in the activity around them. Johnnie, however, merely clung to life; we wished for him, though dreading it, a blessed release from his life of constant pain.

It was now just a few days before Christmas. Carols filled the airwaves. Anticipation filled all the children outside the contagious ward, who so far had shown no signs of illness—not even Colette, who was a pushover for any wandering virus. Part of our prayer was surely answered; all the infections had stayed within their appointed area.

Fortunately, we were able to do our Christmas shopping by telephone, and there were gifts for everyone. Bill and I were exhausted from the past two weeks; the worry and fear, plus the work and lack of sleep, left us drained of energy. All we wanted for Christmas was a good night's sleep.

It was our family custom to hustle the children off to bed early Christmas Eve, then pitch in to set up the pine tree and decorate it and the house—the last touch being the placement of the wee figure of the Christ Child in the manger of the miniature stable. This year Anita and Helenmarie volunteered to play Santa and do the work; we agreed willingly.

We sat back on the sofa, that Christmas Eve, and watched them trim the tree: stringing the colored lights, stretching arm and body to the limit to straighten the star at the top of the tree, putting a ball here and there, stepping back to scrutinize the effect, tilting their heads from right to left. This was the first year we were unaware of our children's secret meetings and the conspiracy that went into planning and making gifts for each member of the family; but the results of the weeks of hard work and trips to the corner store were on the floor. A large pile of gaily, if inexpertly, wrapped gifts had been brought down early in the evening by the youngsters.

Looking at them, Bill whispered to me, "How many genuine handmade hot pads will you get from Santa, would you guess?"

One could feel the excitement of the two girls as they carefully selected each colorful fragile ball to hang on the bushy green tree, whose pungent pine perfume filled the room.

Anita suddenly turned on the stepladder and asked, "Mom, what do you want for Christmas?" She grinned knowingly because somewhere in that pile of packages was a gift already wrapped for me. Closing my eyes I leaned back on the sofa and thought for a moment.

"If I could awake tomorrow and find Robin, Todd, and Johnnie resting comfortably with no fever, I think that's all I really want for Christmas."

We were up long before dawn Christmas morning—a not unusual phenomenon on that feast day. It was a luminous white Christmas; the moonlight shimmered on the snow-coated evergreens and fields of fresh snow.

The house was unusually quiet; there wasn't a cough,

sigh, or moan from the sick rooms. After a last look at the moonlit beauty of the morning outside, I pushed the switch lighting the tree. The warm multicolored lights on the huge scotch pine transformed the room. For one brief moment, I felt only love and happiness could be here; fear and suffering were lost in the shadows.

Flashlight in hand, I quietly made my way to check the sick ones. As I stopped by Kelly's bed a little hand reached out to me and her Christmas greeting was the same as any non-Christmas day, "Hi, Cookie!" she chirped merrily. Next was Todd's room; the beam of the light did not disturb his deep peaceful sleep. I leaned over and felt his forehead; it was cool. He stirred slightly at my touch, then drifted back to renewing sleep; his stormy feverish battle was ended and he had won—again.

Almost fearful, I ventured in to look at Robin and Johnnie. They were so quiet! The light of the flashlight touched Robin; he turned his head away from the sudden brightness. Now I stepped quickly to his side and patted his cheek, a cool cheek; the fever had left him too. I stopped to whisper a Christmas prayer of thanksgiving and meditation: "The wise may call these little ones 'vegetables,' but I love them as I love you, newborn child in a stable manger. The clever men had unspeakable names for you too, Lord."

Johnnie did not waken; his thin emaciated body moved with his breathing, evenly and gently, lifting his blanket rhythmically. He was unaware of time and pain; his fever was gone.

Lord, mine was the best Christmas of all!

～ 14 ～
The Deluge

Todd and Robin were on the mend; ounce by ounce they regained lost weight. Fever had burned Todd's skin; he looked as if he had been under a sunlamp too long, and the skin was peeling from head to toe. There were no other aftereffects. He emerged from his long, hot night as bright, cheerful, and determined to get back to playing as he was before; he was not eager to resume work on his therapy. What little boy does like to work?

Then there was Johnnie—cured of measles and scarlet fever only to continue his dying in agony; a pitiful contradiction.

Several days after Christmas, Johnnie's temperature began to rise and fall erratically. "Nitwit fever," the doctor called it; the body temperature control in Johnnie's brain was damaged by the spreading tumor. The doctor advised us to place him in a hospital if we could.

Since he was an orphan and a ward of Child Welfare in a neighboring county, he would have to be taken to a big hospital in Cleveland. We notified his caseworker, who arranged for his admission and told us to bring the child to the emergency entrance.

It was a cold, gray, Sunday afternoon, the last of December. The roadsides were walled four- to five-feet high with winter's accumulated snow, soot black, ice hard. The road was rough and hazardous with ice patches. From the look of the sky, more snow would be falling soon.

Johnnie slept soundly during the long, slow ride; the

medication he was given before we left was doing its work. We hoped he would sleep until he was settled in a crib at the hospital.

There were lines of people along the corridor we entered after passing through the door marked Emergency. ("Emergency, a situation that requires immediate action"—Webster.) The lines were made up of poor people: some were children, some aged, some white, others black. All appeared miserable; all unsmiling and ill clad. Their poverty was visible, audible, smellable. The faces wore the tight mask of the patience of the poor—the coerced virtue.

Passing these people, we approached a desk set out in the hall where a young man in white was sitting. We told him we had brought Johnnie to be admitted.

"But this is the wrong place; take him to the admitting office."

"This is where the caseworker told us to bring him."

"A welfare case," he sighed, "in that case you'll have to wait your turn."

"Surely, you don't mean we'll have to wait in line with a baby as sick as this one?"

"That's right, lady—should take about two hours, maybe longer, depending on whether they have empty beds upstairs." And with these indifferent words he rose and walked over to a uniformed policeman and began to chat about a football game being played that afternoon.

We were stunned—coerced into a situation never experienced before, we witnessed the treatment given to charity patients. Enduring indifference is one of the indignities the poor suffer daily—the lack of human respect for the person, dismissed as a case.

I was furious at the kind of charity dispensed beneath the large crucifix on the wall. A child might die in your arms or a man drop dead from loss of blood while waiting a turn to be given emergency aid.

"It could be worse," said Bill.

"How?" I asked.

"If we were black."

We had been waiting more than an hour when Johnnie

began to stir in my arms. Soon he was awake, writhing and crying in pain; his parched lips and glazed eyes showed the fever had returned. My patience evaporated as his temperature rose. Johnnie's agonized cries drew all eyes to him. The man in white, who had returned to his desk, showed signs of becoming uncomfortable too, at the shrill sound of incessant, intolerable pain.

"Take him up to the admitting office," he said, "and get the paper work done. By the time that's finished it'll probably be his turn."

It was a relief to get out of that corridor of cases. In the admitting office, we faced the further frustration of trying to fit our emergency case into the inflexibility of paper forms, "Child's name, please," the woman at the desk said.

"Johnnie."

"Father's name, address, and occupation?"

"Unknown!" We tried to explain that we were foster parents; the information was in the records at Child Welfare.

"It's Sunday," she replied, "I won't be able to contact Welfare, so just give me your name and address and occupation."

The information was given dispiritedly; nothing seemed to make sense in this place.

"Do you have hospital insurance?"

"Yes, Blue Cross, family coverage. But it does not cover this child."

"That can be decided later; what is your policy number?"

During this whole inquisition Johnnie was screaming without a moment's letup. Now a woman in white, one of the hospital's sisters, entered the glass cubicle we were in, looked at the screaming child a moment and said, "Let me take this child upstairs—he needs immediate attention."

Our inquisitor gasped at this breach of sacred, red tape, "He's not processed yet; he hasn't been examined in the emergency room; he's a welfare case."

Our savior in white—Sister Joan of Arc, perhaps—cut the protest short by saying, "I'll be responsible if there are questions asked." She motioned to us to follow her.

Upstairs, the ward we entered was large, airy, spotlessly clean; bright printed curtains hung from the windows. Several of the shiny steel beds were empty; on one of these the sister placed Johnnie. Several nurses approached and were told, "Get as much history as you can from his foster mother. Call the floor doctor to examine the child. Any further problems, call me." With that she disappeared as swiftly and quietly as she had appeared.

We left after giving the ward supervisor the information she asked for and Johnnie a farewell kiss. The clock in the hall made us realize that we had been in the hospital more than three hours. Save for the grace of the good nurse, we would have been still in the crowded corridor of the emergency entrance. "Why," we asked each other, "couldn't the others be like her?" A rhetorical—perhaps foolish—question.

We mulled over the question during the slow drive home. Snow was falling, and night came early. Years of rural living and village life had caused us to forget the element of truth in the description of big cities as organized misery. More so, a large hospital in a large city is organized to treat misery and sickness on a large scale. Social scientists claim that the impersonal demeanor of urban life is a respect for the right to privacy; but often it is a hard shell, an aversion to becoming involved. ("Tell your troubles to Jesus, I've got enough of my own.") Often, though, underneath the carapace, the blank, calloused surface, one finds great kindness and goodness, as we did at the hospital that afternoon.

Three weeks later, a January thaw enveloped the land with two nights and days of fog and rain. The temperature was above freezing for the first time since Thanksgiving Day.

During this period, life at home was relaxed; relieved by the thought that Johnnie was getting the best of care at the hospital. Robin and Todd had fully recovered; worry and sleepless nights were forgotten for a while. Todd joined Eric and David on the living room floor building castles and medieval fortresses.

Kelly, slouching in her wheelchair, peered intently, quietly at the boys as they carefully, almost breathlessly, placed blocks on the rising walls. Then, with a well-aimed toss of her doll, she brought the proud towers tumbling down. Her crowing cry of triumph, "Pretty kitty!" could be heard above the anguished wails of the builders. There is no martial music as yet composed that equals the sound of children at play.

Two events, one scheduled, the other falling within that wide category, act of God, occurred to break the tedium of winter. David, age seven, our youngest child, was due for a tonsillectomy; he was to be admitted early in the morning and released the same day. The evening before this unpleasant event took place, the weatherman announced on the newscast that a change in weather was moving from the south into our area; squinting at his isobars and maps, he predicted rain.

"That will be a welcome change; maybe get rid of the snow," we said.

Very early the next morning we could hear the rain as we prepared to leave for the hospital; getting David up was the big chore. He buried his head deeper beneath his blankets as we tugged at him; he had put on an air of bravado the night before, in front of his brothers, but down inside he was scared. I helped him to get his clothes on, while his father was outside starting the car. When he came back into the house he said it was as wet and dark outside as the bottom of a well.

I was glad Bill was driving; he would leave the car at the hospital and take a bus to his office. Visibility was not much above zero; the fog, the pelting rain, the deceptive reflections on pools of water on the pavement, and the distorting refractions from the lights of approaching cars made us dizzy. At times it was impossible to see ahead as windshield wipers failed to keep up with water splashed on the glass from above and below; but, driving slowly, we made it to the hospital.

Our reception at the hospital was in remarkable contrast to the one we had experienced weeks earlier. David and I were ushered immediately to David's hospital room, while Bill answered the standard questions in the admitting office.

I rejoined Bill in the lobby after David fell into a deep sleep, and the nurse assured me that he would not awaken until hours after the operation. "I don't like the looks of the weather. If the rain keeps up this way, and all the snow melts, we'll float away," Bill said. He handed me the car key, and added, "You'd better drive home this afternoon to make sure that all is well. I'll meet you here at the hospital after work." He left to catch a bus.

I settled down with a magazine, hours of waiting ahead of me. At nine o'clock I walked to the window and looked out; it was still dark and the rain poured down. There was something eerie about darkness in the middle of the morning. A breath of the fog and rain chilled my heart; vague apprehensions about David and the children at home made me restless.

By the light of the street lamps, I could see rushing water overflowing the curbs and coming to a boil at the overfilled catch basins. I tried to brush worry aside—que sera, sera—but merely strengthened it.

Around noon, after drinking a cup of coffee in the cafeteria, I looked in on David again. He was sleeping serenely, not yet aware of the loss of his tonsils. The nurse caring for him assured me that his condition was normal, and that it would be several hours before he was fully conscious. I decided to drive home and check on things there. My fast sprint outdoors, from hospital door to the car in the parking lot, took long enough for the rain to drench me. Though it was past noon, there was barely enough daylight to see the car. Objects—even the piles of ice which remained as monuments of winter's might—appeared luminous gray framed with dark edges.

Beyond the suburbs, the road became a stream, but I did not realize what was happening until the water rose above, or the car sank below, the floor level in a slight dip in the road. The engine stalled. Now what?

No cars or human beings in sight; several houses nearby, but nothing to show whether the occupants were at home. I hugged my knees, my feet on the seat, above the intruding water. What now?

Impatience, as the minutes dragged by, made the prospect of braving the cold water outside a lesser evil; and I was about to push the door open and get out to look for help when, in the rearview mirror, I saw a car approaching. I opened a window and leaned out, waving my arm frantically. The driver was a man, and he came to a stop slowly. I shouted to him to call a tow truck; whether he heard me I didn't know, but he backed his car, turned, and headed back.

I closed the window and resumed my former position and patient frame of mind, freshened by hope of rescue. Finally, a red and white tow truck eased up behind the car and pushed it until I was on high ground. After a faster push, the car's engine started. I paid the good Samaritan his reasonable charge; he warned me to be on the lookout for low areas and suggested taking an alternate route home. Shaken now and fearful, I thanked him and followed his advice.

Seen from far up the road, our house appeared much as a lighthouse completely surrounded by water. The fog and rain added to the sense of unreality. Slowing the car to a crawl, I drove through the water, which was about a foot deep. As I turned into our driveway, navigating by the two lamp posts there, I noticed big slabs of ice floating over the lawn. Probably they came from the pond—ice on which the children had been skating only three days before.

I stopped the car as near the side entrance to the house as possible. Entering, I breathed a sigh of thanks on being there. As I shut the door, I heard the sound of water cascading into deep pools; opening the door to the basement, I saw dirty, brown water. Boxes, pieces of wood, and clothing were floating around.

Then I had to laugh. Descending two steps, I saw two creatures, grotesquely attired, moving around in the knee-deep water. One was Anita, our petite Titi, in her Dad's hip boots; the other was Gert, my dependable, alternate foster mother, in high boots also. They were absorbed in their mission of salvage. They were surprised to see me;

piqued too, perhaps, by my laughter. What's funny? was their expression as they waded toward me. Then, sitting on the upper steps, we all began to laugh.

One thing was clear: shedding tears would not dry the basement. As we sat on the cellar steps, there was a slight masochistic pleasure in pointing out to each other the damage: that the gas furnace, as well as the hot water heater, was half under water. That meant no heat and no hot water; the electric clothes dryer, which Anita and Gert had managed to lift to the top of a table, was now floating about, table and all.

I recalled the sump pump. "What happened to the sump pump?" I asked Gert.

"It was running when we first came down," she said. "But it's not pumping out any water."

I phoned Bill. He said he would catch the next bus and be home in an hour and a half. I insisted he tell me how to get the pump to work; thousands of gallons could be pumped in one and a half hours.

He agreed and said that probably the discharge line was frozen. The most likely spot would be halfway from the outside basement wall to the attached garage in the crawlspace under the playroom.

Returning to the basement stairway, I instructed Anita. "Wade carefully back to daddy's workbench and, if it is still there, bring me the hacksaw."

"But, mom," she protested, "what's the hacksaw look like, and what do you want it for?"

"Just bring me the first small saw you find on the bench." I didn't know what a hacksaw looked like either.

When she sloshed back, I pointed to a plastic pipe which rose from the floor and, about a foot below the ceiling, disappeared into the wall. I explained, "That pipe runs under Michael's playroom and then goes into the ground to the sewer line. I'm going to cut that pipe with his saw. That will let the water run into the garage and then outdoors."

"*You* are?" Gert asked incredulously.

I dashed outdoors to get to the garage. The incessant rain splashed my face. Once inside, I removed the yard-square door in the garage wall giving access to the crawl-space; it was dark, cold, and musty under there; I could feel the cobwebs clinging to my face and arms. I crawled awkwardly, a flashlight in one hand and a saw in the other, over the cement floor that seemed to be strewn with gravel.

I found the pipe and with immense optimism began sawing—who needs a man for every little emergency around the house? The saw cut the plastic quickly. Then it happened; water burst from the severed pipe. In a second I was drenched and battered. I scurried out, across the wet concrete. Before I re-entered the house, I put on an air that I hoped would seem brave.

"Don't worry about the basement; everything will be all right. I cut the pipe and the water is pouring out of the garage."

But the problem wasn't solved. This was no ordinary rain, and an extraordinary amount of accumulated snow was melting; water flowed in faster than it could be pumped out. We could see French Creek (a quarter mile away) overflowing its banks and spreading toward us.

I called our neighbor, who lived in a basementless house, and asked him to help; he came with his son and lifted our vulnerable electric appliances to a higher level. Nothing could be done for the furnace; I asked him to shut the main gas valve at the meter.

Anita had turned on the radio and heard a special weather bulletin; rain would continue until late evening or early morning. Large areas were flooded; some roads were impassable due to high water; families in low areas were being evacuated.

Within an hour our friendly creek had flooded the highway. From the upstairs sun porch, one is able to view a vast area. As I looked that afternoon, the familiar scene had suffered a sea-change; the woods and meadows were submerged into a weird, gray seascape, a Netherlands without dikes; over it all the rain kept falling. I recalled that David was in the hospital and most certainly awake and desperately wanting his mother; it was apparent that I dare not drive there.

I called his godmother, whose home was near the hospital; she volunteered to go immediately, stay with David, and take him to her home in the evening when he was released. We discovered later that he was more heartsick than throatsick, because he had to miss all the excitement of the flood.

When Bill finally arrived home, much later than he had expected, he surveyed the situation and said, "The only serious problem is keeping the house warm for the children."

Eric, Colette, and Sue vehemently resisted all suggestions of going to a friend's or relative's house, just when the fun and excitement were beginning. Anita and Helenmarie persuaded us they could bundle up to keep warm for the night.

Todd, who usually enjoyed going visiting, frowned, stuck out his lower lip, and shook his head vigorously to the suggestion that he spend the night elsewhere. Nobody was going to take him away from this wonderful flood which he had been watching from a window all afternoon.

We went on with our nightly chores of feeding and preparing the babies for bed, meanwhile concealing our fears and praying that the rain would end. By midnight all was quiet; rain no longer pelted the windows; no sound of traffic came from the road; and the glow of the red flash of the patrol car, which was directing traffic to alternate routes, appeared brighter—no longer frightening but holiday red. At 2:30 A.M., Bill noticed a slight drop in the water level of the basement. Since this was an indication that the cresting of the creek had past, I suggested we try to get some sleep.

Up again early the next morning, we could see the stars, and they were inspiring. From the high-water mark, plain on the basement walls, we established that the water had fallen two feet while we slept. The temperature in the babies' rooms had held at 70°. This good news and hot coffee encouraged us to face the coming day cheerfully. The sun arose on the horizon revealing the cluttered damage of the flood.

We brought David home next evening. Johnnie was

released from the hospital four weeks later, when the first harbingers of spring were appearing. But his cries now were feeble, his waking hours less frequent. Late one evening, when the house was unusually quiet—the older children being at a school play and the younger ones asleep—I heard a long sigh from Johnnie's room. In the dim light of the night lamp, I could see that for him life and pain had reached an end.

~ 15 ~
A Word from JFK

Awaited eagerly every day by families on any rural postal route is the arrival of the mail carrier in his dust-covered, mud-splattered, right-hand-drive vehicle; seldom did it pass us without a stop. It was a dull day when the mailbox yielded only bills and box-holder ads. Usually there was a letter from one of our friends or our daughters' pen pals or from Todd's Aunt Sue (a most faithful correspondent who lived in the state of Washington).

Colette had been receiving a good deal of important looking mail, in embossed envelopes, hand addressed. One morning Eric ran into the house with a whoop. "A letter for Chichi from the White House!"

Trembling with excitement, Colette carefully opened the envelope; out slipped a note with the greeting: All the best wishes. It was signed John F. Kennedy.

This one-line note became her most precious treasure. It was the chief prize among the letters she received from Queen Elizabeth of England, in Buckingham Palace; from David Brinkley, handwritten; from Chet Huntley along with an autographed photo. Each letter Colette mounted in a large scrapbook that was repeatedly brought out to show to anyone she could corner.

This influx of mail from the great and the near great was the result of a letter-writing spree which began as a school project for Colette. She seemed to have been born with a love of reading, as Eric was with a love for music. As a preschooler, she lugged around volumes of fairy tales and books of verse, always on the lookout for some one to read to her; later she pretended to read to her juniors, Eric and David, by repeating stories she had memorized.

It was the biggest thrill of her life when the school doors opened to her. She was first out of bed in the morning, first in the front yard waiting for the yellow school bus. But the pressure of school life seemed to increase the number and severity of her black-out spells. Not only was she falling in the playgrounds, on the school bus, and in the halls, but even at her desk. She blotted out the teacher's instructions, which led to weird interpretations of her studies. She was drifting into a semiamnesic state and felt frustrated when she failed to give the right answer.

In spelling, handwriting, and reading (at least in word recognition), she did well. She could read a passage beautifully, with feeling. But when she had finished, she could not recall what she had read.

Her favorite game was playing school. She set up a rough facsimile of a classroom in her room, and daily, by hoax or coax, she gathered David, Todd, Kelly, and her dolls to attend the classes she taught. It was amusing to see David with a French dictionary upside down, but not funny to catch Kelly tearing pages from a volume of Japanese color prints.

Class in session, Colette—adopting one of teacher's "dirty looks" and fault-finding voice—would reenact a day at school. It might have proved instructive for a teacher to watch. She wrote on the blackboard and gave spelling tests to which only David could respond. She drew pictures for her pupils and read from her reader. Alternately she scolded and praised them, graded their papers and passed out report cards.

School was her great love and at the same time her greatest frustration. She strove for perfection, practicing her penmanship until she achieved a fine, neat handwriting; she sought that same perfection in her reading and arithmetic, but the concentration needed was constantly short-circuited by her spells. The harder she tried, the more she blacked out; and the more baffled she became, the more blackouts—a truly vicious circle.

Unaware as she was of the onset and duration of her spells, Colette was made painfully aware of their existence by bruises and lacerations on her body. She was left out of games on the playground because of her falls; she stood alone on the sideline, watching with eyes that held back tears. Finally the doctor told us emphatically that she would have to be withdrawn from school.

He advised us to apply for a home tutor. Colette must have no pressure on her; she was to work at her own pace and not feel compelled to keep up with others.

When we told Colette, her spirit was crushed. A part of her died that day. We were weighted down with a feeling of guilt of betrayal. We tried to point out the fun she would have with her very own teacher; that she would use the same books and receive the same report cards the other kids did.

Her teacher came to the house twice a week. Colette settled down to learning, but she lacked the old enthusiasm, the gaiety and excitement of school.

We were not convinced that this was the best answer to Colette's problem, for her blackouts continued. One consoling aspect was that she now was close by and could be guarded. We anticipated unsafe situations, hazardous areas and furnishings. We became aware that a pencil or paint brush could become a stiletto if she fell on it; but hope—that priceless ingredient of life—supported us as we strove for a rational balance.

Hope accompanied us on each visit to the doctor: wishful thoughts that a new miracle drug, a new miracle machine in surgery, or something, previously undiscovered, would turn up in these weekly medical sessions.

Hope sustained us as we wrote to every known school for the handicapped or exceptional child—every school listed in a national catalog, from Massachusetts to Minnesota. Each answer was a heartbreaking, disappointing, negative response. Some schools were filled, with waiting lists of applicants for years ahead. Some stated that children with neurological disturbances were not accepted. A few sent application forms, but the cost of tuition, room, and board were so high that we simply tossed these into the wastepaper basket.

In a nearby community, there was a class for slow learners. We approached our county nurse, hoping she could get Colette into it. We were turned away; our daughter had normal intelligence and therefore did not qualify for the group. We appealed to the social service agencies for advice; they could give us none.

It was a problem of tagging (classifying) a handicap. For those with a visible, obvious handicap and for children with mental retardation, society was beginning to stretch out a helping hand. But for a child with a phantom handicap, there seemed no place; it was too indefinite an illness. Children like our daughter belonged neither with the normal nor the handicapped youngsters. They stood aside, alone, waiting for someone in authority to pin a tag on them.

Among our sunny days was the one when a new tutor for Colette arrived, a most likeable, remarkable woman. Jane E. had formerly taught in the local school system, until the care of her own three youngsters occupied all her time.

Colette promptly fell in love with her. From then on it was: "Mrs. E. said I should do it this way, Mrs. E. said that"—and for Colette it was infallible.

Jane made no attempt to force her pupil into the approved pattern but rather molded and modified the system to the fragile capability of her pupil. Intuitively she devised novel ways to reach the child, meantime nurturing a love of learning, opening a window on the wonders of the world. Learning should begin with delight and flourish in wonder, otherwise it is drudgery.

The classroom was at first the dining room; then it moved to Colette's bedroom; finally, a special room was reserved as a classroom only. A heavy, slated blackboard was mounted on one wall, a cork panel on another to hold prize papers with a gold star, bulletins, maps. It has been in use ever since: after Colette was graduated, Todd's classes continued there. Bookshelves and a desk for an electric typewriter were built in later.

Colette brightened and glowed in her new school. Mrs. E. quickly comprehended Colette's spells and when they occurred waited for her full recovery. Then she carefully retraced the lesson until Colette showed recognition of the point at which she had broken away.

When Colette tired of a subject, it was dropped for that day, and a less demanding one was substituted.

There were art classes and handicrafts; geography took on a new dimension with pictures and slides shown from a projector borrowed from the school.

In English class Colette wrote letters to specific persons: former classmates and friends. She was an enthusiastic observer of the political scene, especially through the eyes of Huntley and Brinkley. So it was that she wrote to them and received replies. England and Monaco were not just names on a map but the homes of her friends, Queen Elizabeth and Prince Rainier (and she had letters from them to prove it).

The time now between classes didn't drag; the hours were filled with reading, writing, drawing, cutting, pasting—and waiting for letters.

~ 16 ~
The Baseball Fan

As time passed it became clear that Kelly, Robin, and Michael had reached their peak levels of achievement, physically and mentally. Five-year-old Robin was still unable to move voluntarily; he was still difficult to feed. But he was a lovable boy, always ready with a wide smile for every word and favor and eager, so it seemed, to be able to bring a ray of happiness as his contribution to our family life. He was still plagued with periodic respiratory infections, although less frequently. His body thinned and lengthened; his wavy, brown hair, as it thickened, caused his face to appear fuller than it really was.

Kelly, now able to sit and scoot around the floor on her bottom, had been taken to the Rehabilitation Clinic for evaluation. We hoped that some therapy might help her to stand and possibly walk. Many trips later it was decided that such attempts were useless; her mind was too slow to cooperate—it was all just fun for this fun-one.

Training her to sit was fairly easy; it merely took perseverance with repeated and prolonged sitting sessions. Her back was strong and straight, and her head, though large, was manageable. But standing was another story: her feet were tiny and deformed, her legs rigid and out of line with her hips.

Prescribing leg braces for her was discussed, but the idea was quickly dismissed. Braces, to Kelly, would simply be another challenge to her strength and her uncanny ability to take things off and apart; they would become lethal weapons in her hands, flying projectiles, a danger to anyone in the line of fire.

Elfin Michael, it seemed, never changed. There was no apparent growth in size, vertical or horizontal. He was enigmatic, fiercely independent, continually flitting about his playroom or the screened porch in mild weather. Following labyrinthine patterns, his lonely mind fulfilled his needs.

Only twice in the time he was with us did Michael show any need of another; in both instances he was in an exhausted, weeping state when he sought a lap and comforting. I held him close and rocked him, and the tensions drained from his quivering muscles.

Absentmindedly I asked, "How about giving mommy a kiss?" I never expected any response. Mirabile dictu, he raised his head and touched my cheek with a light dewdrop kiss; my heart rose and choked me. And I recalled the words of one doctor: "We can never be sure of what really goes on in their little heads; perhaps, they just don't know how to communicate."

This show of emotion he repeated only once; otherwise, he wanted to be left alone.

Todd's progress was another story. He went twice a week for physical and speech therapy at the Cerebral Palsy Rehabilitation Center, ten miles from home. The orthopedic specialist and therapists were encouraging in their reports; above all they enjoyed working with Todd, because he was so cooperative and determined.

He was fitted with steel braces from shoulders to toes; encased in these, he could stand erect at his standing-table and could hold his otherwise jerking and drooping body straight. He wore as much iron as a Norman knight, which made it awkward to dress him. We looked forward to the day when he could stand and sit without braces—perhaps, even walk.

Bill constructed a set of parallel bars and between them Todd struggled to move his rigid body step by step. It was agonizing to watch him concentrate and try to control his hands, in order not to lose his grip on the bars and slip and fall. Every ounce of his energy was drawn upon as he attempted to make his whole body work at once.

It tired us merely to watch him: beads of sweat rolled down his face, and his lower lip was thrust out with bulldog tenacity. His conscious will sought to impose order on his disorganized reflexes.

Todd was no quitter; whenever he lost his grip and pitched forward, he would look up from the floor with a big grin and nod when asked if he wanted to try again.

He had a small tricycle, to which we welded a solid steel back brace which encircled his chest to hold him upright. With his feet strapped to the pedals, he would try to wheel about the house.

Here again, when he had control of one limb, the opposite leg or arm would strike out in reverse, sending him weaving in every direction, banging into furniture.

All of this activity was a part of Todd's therapy, which was to strengthen his muscles and coordinate his movements. With each piece of equipment, our expectations rose, as though each were a magic wand which would enable him to walk and run. We were puzzled vaguely at his slow progress physically but were reassured after speaking with the doctors and therapists.

"It takes a long time with cerebral palsy," they'd say, and Todd would grin and grind his teeth in a show of determination. Actually, though, the harder he tried the more tense he got; the more tense he got the more spastic and helpless he became. Gradually we learned from watching his efforts that the secret to success was relaxing.

Over and over again I'd say, "Relax, take a deep breath, make yourself feel like an old rag doll, and then try again."

This was a hard thing for him to do, because he was in a hurry for success.

Todd's mind was quick; by the time he was five he was an avid (or is it rabid?) baseball fan. He had learned the game by watching it on television along with our youngsters. With every run batted in by the home team, he would thrust his body backwards, pushing on his footrests. After a winning season—rare for our team— the leather back of the chair was as worn and scuffed as Mickey Mantle's glove.

A night Todd will never forget is the one we took him and David to the stadium to watch the Indians and Red Sox play. He had been given four tickets, so David, Bill, and I were his guests. It was a beautiful evening in June, clear and warm, with just enough lake breeze to keep us comfortable and aid the soaring flight of fly balls.

A wheelchair has its advantages at times; we were allowed to drive right up to the entrance gate and given preferred-parking space for a quick exit. Dave and I pushed Todd into the stadium and up the ramp near our section; having instructed David to wait at that spot, I returned to the main entrance and awaited Bill, who was parking the car.

When we rejoined David and Todd, they were in an animated conversation with two tweedy strangers who seemed delighted with Todd's excitement. One of the men introduced himself, "I'm a sports writer, ma'am" (he mentioned the paper, which I forget). "I cover the Red Sox; and Bob, here, is in public relations for the Indians. We've been having a little talk with your sons; I understand Todd is a real fan, and Herb Score and Rocky Colavito are his heroes."

The boys grinned and twisted in delight.

"Where will you be sitting?" the Boston scribe asked. Bill showed our tickets; the two strangers then left, promising to see us later.

We found our seats and settled down. The lights were already on, though the sun had not yet set; the grass on the field was a bright green, and the contrast with the base paths and pitcher's mound made a pleasing design. Todd was ecstatic with this vision, and with the sight of the thousands of people, and the sound of the hawkers of beer, pop, and programs.

The grounds keepers were busy brushing up invisible specks. The umpires in their clerical black were solemnly engaged in talk. I always wonder what they talk about: their health, the wages, the latest umpire joke? David and Todd were enthralled at how different the real thing looked from the televised one—the substance from the shadow, the panorama from the peek.

David rattled off a litany of questions that could be heard by the occupants of seats a dozen rows away. Then our friends from the press reappeared with all sorts of surprises. With them was Herb Score, who gave Todd an autographed baseball. The sports scribe from

Boston handed him a ball autographed by all the players in the dugouts, pictures of all the players, and their autographs.

The boys were speechless.

The band struck up the national anthem, and everyone, except Todd, stood up. Then we heard, "Play ball!" The home team won; twice the scoreboard exploded with fireworks, saluting a home run; topping off a perfect evening was a fireworks display after the game.

Exhausted from his exhilarating experiences, Todd curled up beside us in the car and dropped off to sleep, his treasured baseballs tightly locked in his arms. It had amazed us to discover his grasp of the game, his recognition of each player, how swiftly he had indicated answers to David's questions, and how he had corrected Bill, by vigorously shaking his noggin, on an answer to one of David's queries. If his physical progress could only match his mental abilities, I thought what an athlete he'd become!

Despite his snail-paced physical progress (muscular control), Todd's grim determination to achieve was a daily thrill to watch. He was a real champ, an inspiration. Despite an almost impossible handicap, he was a worker, a fighter, filled with a gay, laughing, emotional balance which more than compensated for his lack of physical equilibrium.

Why wasn't he making much progress; what causes cerebral palsy in the first place; why were the others, Kelly, Michael, and Robin, born the way they were; what was wrong with Colette?

Over and over those questions richocheted about our minds. Every book which dealt with some aspect of the problems involved we bought or borrowed. We drove hundreds of miles attending lectures and discussion groups and read and collected articles published in newspapers and periodicals.

One book especially helped us, not because it gave us the answers, but it provided encouragement; it inspired us to keep trying, not to give up. The name of the book is *Karen* written by Marie Killilea, Karen's mother. We found this remarkable story power-packed with keen insights and the hope that one needs more than anything else to face the reality of a child seriously handicapped.

The more information we absorbed, the greater became the realization of how little was known about the brain-damaged child. Likewise, we became sadly aware that what was hailed as a medical breakthrough one year was quietly rejected as worthless the next. Every few weeks, it seemed, a medical miracle was announced by the news media; the demise of the patient a few days later was noted only in the obituary column, if at all.

In our own experience with Colette and Todd, we were always encouraged by a few vague references by the doctors, holding out the hope of a new drug being developed, a new surgical technique which would correct the child's disabilities.

~17~
State School for the Retarded

What happens to exceptional children as they grow older? We made inquiries, and the common answer was, "they were probated" (declared mentally incompetent by a judge of probate court) and became wards of the state upon reaching six years of age.

We decided to visit our state hospital (or School for the Retarded, as it was called).

It was mid-August when we went there. It had been a beautiful summer with a sufficient rainfall to keep lawns a fresh green and flower beds bursting with color. We left early in the morning; it was a four-hour drive to the state capital from our home. The drive was restful and relaxing; it was a relief to get a break from daily chores and noisy demands of children.

Traffic was light and the rural countryside delightful: well-kept farmland and woodlots, huge red barns and white houses, herds of cattle at pasture, and hawks wheeling high in the blue sky. All was beautiful that day.

Billboards, automobile graveyards, and a growing number of seedy service stations signaled the approach to the city, whose narrow streets we had to traverse before we reached the state hospital. The hospital was set far back from the road and was composed of groups of ancient, dark buildings: a high iron fence surrounded the place.

We turned in at the first driveway. Despite well-manicured lawns and gardens, there was a forbidding aura about the place. Inside the high-ceilinged entrance hall, with its dark, heavy woodwork, the walls seemed to press in on us; one felt suffocated breathing the air, a compound of dry-rot dust, mould, and floor polish. There was no one to be seen, but muffled voices could be heard behind closed doors.

One of the doors opened, and a young man entered quietly; when he saw us standing hesitantly, he inquired if he could help us. We began explaining our purpose; he interrupted to tell us we were in the wrong building. The school for retarded children was down the road. The building we were in was the hospital for the mentally ill.

It was a keen relief to leave this dark place and breathe fresh air. Walking to the car, we felt hundreds of eyes watching from rows of steel-grated windows above. On the short drive to the school, groups of boys working in the gardens stared at us curiously—young patients, perhaps. The school was similar in style to the hospital we had just left—the same high ceilings and dark woodwork—but here, there was more visible activity. Doors were open and office personnel were at desks. Typewriters were clacking. Bright-printed chintz drapes on windows and a vase of flowers on a desk added splashes of color.

As we waited, we studied the contents of an old display cabinet, a few pieces of needlework, products, probably, of some long ago occupational therapy class. Wrinkled and faded, they looked as though they had been placed there years ago and forgotten.

We had a letter of introduction written by the friend of a friend, who had political prestige of some sort; it was addressed to a social worker at the school, a young man in a dark suit, heavy horn-rimmed glasses, brush haircut—giving us the impression of having met him somewhere before.

"I'll show you the cottages first," he said, "and then the new school." He led us through corridors and down a long flight of stairs. Outside we went toward a group of roofed, one-story buildings; our guide explained that these were fairly new, modern cottages built to accommodate various age groups, sex groups, handicapped groups.

The nearer we came to the cottages, the more apparent became the atmosphere of neglect. Lawns were overgrown and infested with buckthorn; there were no gardens.

Outside of one cottage stood the skeletons of playground equipment. Bars meant to hold six swings were empty save one lone chain with a swing seat dragging on the ground; steel supports for teeter-totters had no seesaw planks.

Small groups of boys stood about, listless; some of the boys stared into space, a few smiled a shy greeting, one asked for a cigarette. We came upon solitary figures, here and there, hunched up, arms hugging knees, heads drooped—dark blobs of human dejection incarnate.

The first sense of shock on entering the cottage was suffered by our noses. The interior reminded us of a cow barn. The floor was of concrete. In wheelchairs and on benches were young men, or shells of men; they seemed devoid of animation, expressionless. On a high shelf, a small television set flickered through a sequence of a quiz program; the emcee's fruity voice and the canned laughter sounded obscene in this dreadful place. No one paid any attention to it. The patients' clothes were shabby and ill-fitting; mismatched shoes on sockless feet; and over all, the air was heavy with the smell of unwashed, soiled clothing and body odors.

Our guide impassively led us to the next room; here we were met by a woman in a white uniform. She received us graciously and immediately showed us the room where the drugs were kept; these, she explained, were tranquilizers, vitamins, and anticonvulsive drugs. Then she took us to see the children whose muffled voices we had heard from the adjoining room.

Selecting a key from an enormous ring clipped to her waist, she opened a door. A blast of sickening, foul air struck us; and a herd of naked little people rushed toward us. There were at least seventy-five of them. Their skin was pallid; many had sores; some had their hands tied behind their backs. A few outstretched arms were thrust at us, begging; we regretted not bringing candy and cookies; how hungry they looked! Thin arms clung to my skirt, and all about us in this barnlike building, with its concrete floors and steelgrated windows, milled boys. Some were eager and responsive, but most were little boys with that faraway, lost look about them. Little boys.

"Oh God," I thought, "the animals in our metropolitan zoo receive better care—the zoo is most certainly cleaner."

In every face I could see a Michael or a Kelly, and the horror of it made me want to run from this storage bin of small, helpless human beings.

"It's such a beautiful day; why can't they go outdoors to play?" I asked the attendant.

"I just don't have help to take them out."

I remembered the one broken swing and overgrown lawn, and I knew they never went out.

We walked to an adjoining room; it was filled with cots. There was barely enough space between the cots to walk; each held a mattress but no sheet or pillow or blanket. In this room, as in the other, there was no trace of color, no toys—ball, block, or game. Here everything was gray: complexions, mood, floor, walls, mattresses; no flowered chintz drapes on the windows here, no bright prints on the walls, no gay mobiles suspended from the ceiling, nothing in sight or touch in which a child could find joy. No sound of music. At least, music could have been piped in; music to sway and dance to, as even the youngest child will naturally do.

Fury choked me at the sight of this total indignity stamped on helpless children—the spiritual rape that was their daily routine. Tears burned my eyes. All I wanted was to run from this horror, this too real, Dickensian nightmare.

Our guide was not finished with the tour. "The next cottage is for bed patients," he explained as we entered another barn which was filled with row after row of cribs and cots, each holding a silent victim.

These were the severe cases—the total cases like Robin. Not a whimper nor sigh came from these emaciated bodies; as we passed each crib we saw the plastic tubes that kept them alive—barely alive; these were the tube-fed children. Flies were crawling over the faces of the unconscious ones, resting on the open sores of others. Our eyes were drawn to the open windows. No screens.

Nausea came in waves, black waves of guilt. The cottages were filled with our nothingness; our gray lack of love suffocating us with the smells of lingering death.

Outside I gulped fresh air. I had had it; I didn't want to see more, but our guide didn't want us to miss seeing the new school building. This was some distance from the cottage area; the fresh air and the sight of blue skies revived me as we walked along the path.

We passed a tall, dark, fortresslike edifice. I observed many broken windows.

"What is this building?" I asked.

"That is for the older boys. I don't think I'll have time to show you that one," he quickly said.

I felt chilled with the surmise of why he did not want us to see what was behind those broken windows.

The classroom building that our guide wanted us to see was a modern, sprawling, brick structure with large windows and glass doors. It was surprisingly quiet when we entered—a decided contrast: light, airy, empty. It was sparkling clean, cheerful, and colorful.

We were introduced to a small elderly woman, a veteran teacher; she was kind and seemed dedicated. She, as well as the few attendants we had met, were valiant women struggling against impossible conditions.

Equipment and help were in short supply—"cuts in the budget, you know, year after year." The building was beautiful but was merely wasted space, with not enough teachers to man the classrooms.

Our tour was over; we had seen only a few of many buildings. After thanking our host, we found our way back to the parking lot, and as we wound our way through the vast complex of buildings, unvisited, ancient ones, I shivered.

~ 18 ~
Give Love Away

The emetic memory of the state school remained with me like the ache of a guilty conscience. I wished I had never seen the place, never seen this continuing sin against helpless children. I reproached myself for the wish. It was an attempt to hide as a faceless statistic within an anonymous society, as one of the three monkeys—the one hiding his eyes.

Rationalizing, I made myself believe that some stroke of good fortune would prevent Robin from leaving us and going to that place. He was now five and a half; when he reached his sixth birthday in early spring, he would be probated and his name placed on the waiting list for admission to the school.

Our impressions of the state institution we kept to ourselves, but gradually we let it be known to our children that Robin would be leaving us. To them, Robin had been through so much, so close to death so many times, that thoughts of his leaving seemed unreal. "Aw, don't worry, mom," eleven-year-old Eric said, trying to comfort me, "Robbie belongs with us—nobody'll take him away."

It was early winter (or late fall) and I was housecleaning. I took on the major job of the boys' room. Furniture was pulled out, and from dark corners, under beds, and behind bureaus, I uncovered hidden treasures and piled them on the beds. Kites, long-lost arrows, marbles, playing cards, a box with skeletal remains of some small animal, odd stones, an Indian arrowhead found at French Creek—it was all valuable junk, and as I stood looking at the mound on each bed, perplexed about what to do, the telephone rang.

"This is Dr. H——," a voice said. "I understand that you care for handicapped children in your home. Would you have room for a newborn infant until arrangements could be made to place this baby in an institution?"

Johnnie's bed stood empty. We had never put it away. My reply was an instant yes.

Three days later Susan, five days old, arrived. Her appearing on this cold winter afternoon was like a daffodil pushing through snow. She was a bundle of pale yellow, nestled in the nurse's arms. When the soft blanket was lifted from her face I exclaimed in utter surprise, "She's beautiful! There can't be anything wrong with her; she looks perfect."

The doctor shook his head slightly, saying, "She is a mongoloid." And after a pause, "It's a pity."

When I took this beautiful infant from the nurse I could feel that she was different. She did not curl up as a newborn child does but was limp. As I held her I was spellbound with her delicacy. I lifted her tiny hands and caressed her soft pink cheeks. Her head was covered with fine, golden blond down, that curled gently on her forehead.

The doctor's voice broke the spell. "This," he said, "is her formula," handing me a slip of paper. "Care for her and love her the same way you do a normal child. She has a heart murmur, but that shouldn't cause her any trouble now. Her parents will contact you; in the meantime, if anything should come up that would cause you concern, call me." With that he and the nurse left.

The door was barely closed when the sound of running feet, above me, broke the silence. Down the stairs pounded six youngsters bursting with curiosity. They had all been upstairs in their rooms obediently and quietly studying. Now they stood around the crib ohing and ahing, "She's so tiny!"

David piped up with, "What's its name?"

"Susan, "I replied.

"Oh, my gosh," said Helenmarie, "we've got two Suzies now. What will we do?"

"That's easy," Eric said, "we'll have a Little Sue and a Big Sue," with emphasis on the word big.

This brought a swift, prim reply from his older sister, "Just call me Suzanne, which is my name, you know, and call the baby, Susan; that is her name."

And so we did for a while, but mostly it was Baby Sue. As her temporary stay turned into a more permanent one, we did call her Little Sue and our Sue was prefixed with the word *big* until she joined a missionary religious order and became Sister Sue.

Weeks passed and our small guest stayed on. Her parents' work involved almost constant travelling, and for that reason, they considered it wise to leave the baby in a permanent home.

It was an agonizing decision for them; they loved their baby, wanted her with them, but did what they thought best for her. They joined the fellowship of parents of exceptional children who are constantly plagued by feelings of guilt and frustration, and who are the target, often, of much thoughtless, unjustified criticism.

One of the barbs aimed at us was, "Don't you have enough with your own six?" One teacher asked me openly, "Do you think it's fair to your children?" If these questions had been prompted by behavior problems, or poor academic achievement on the children's part, perhaps the remarks would be called for, but all the youngsters were straight A in conduct, and average or above in scholastic work.

They were normal kids who loved all the normal activities and interests suitable for their ages. If anything, this foster family gave them the best education they could possibly get; it taught them to share, to be patient, kind, and compassionate. It taught them also the fundamentals of child care for the handicapped—invaluable for Anita, who later was to become a nurse, and for Helenmarie as a Peace Corps volunteer, teaching the retarded in San Salvador. What's more, it taught Todd (and later Little Sue and a line of others) that he was a child just like David and Eric, but with a handicap. Had it not been for their acceptance, their drawing him into all their activities and fun, Todd would have resigned himself to be a hopeless cripple.

Often, when I watched them going out to play, the words of a song came to mind:

A bell isn't a bell until you ring it,
A song isn't a song until you sing it,
And love isn't love until you give it away.

Various opinions on our uncommon family floated our way from friends and relatives—opinions mildly pro or violently con: "though I can't see why they take in cripples instead of healthy, normal kids," "it isn't fair to your own children," and "you have enough with your sick Colette."

No one, to our knowledge, accused us of sentimentalism, thank goodness. Perhaps the realization of the tough daily routine of caring for a handicapped child ruled that out. It was no one-shot, one-day, altruistic gesture, such as a Christmas party for the shut-ins or a crippled children's day at the circus.

It was an essay in futility to try to explain our actions, our thoughts, our feelings. For ourselves we were certain that each one of these foster children was meant for our family. We did not go looking for these children; they were brought to us.

Our faith supported our actions: If one does not love his neighbor, he cannot love God. (These unwanted waifs are our neighbors.) "Whatever you did to these least of my brethren you did to me. Whatsoever you did not do for these least, neither did you do it for me," Christ said.

One particular, critical barb touched a sensitive spot: we might be neglecting our own children to care for the sons and daughters of strangers. This aspect we had long ago worried to pieces before we finally buried it; there was simply no truth in it.

Other mothers had outside interests; some were joiners, giving time and energy to raise money for worthy causes and organizations; others chose dressmaking, gardening, painting, or ceramic art. Many mothers worked at full or part-time jobs; I could not see why it was extraordinary or blameworthy of me if I chose, as a hobby and avocation, the care and love of a few extra needy children.

One fine day in May I saw from the kitchen window Eric and David pushing Todd. The wheelchair was piled, in every inch of space, with lumber, saws, hammers, and Todd. A pail of nails dangled from one handle of the chair.

They were on the way to work on their new project, a tree house high in a huge, black oak tree, a noble tree with a girth of fourteen feet.

"Aren't they rushing the season a bit?" I asked Sue, who was sifting flour into a bowl—a mask of white dust covered her face. "Already they're begging to sleep out nights."

"Heck, no, mom. You should see the loot they have stored up there," she confided as she began whipping away at a cake. "They have their sleeping bags, flashlight, a bunch of comic books, and extra blankets."

"How do you know all this?"

"Oh! Well, it was so beautiful the other night, that when every one was sleeping, Helenmarie and I slipped out and slept up there. It was scary but fun."

One could only wonder what other secrets were in their little heads. I later learned that the boys took Todd to their aerie; I shudder still at the thought of his being lofted up their rickety ladder. But I said nothing. A child must find it tiresome to be continually told, "Do this," and "Don't do that."

Even adults, especially parents, get plenty of dos and don'ts, you shoulds, and you shouldn'ts—advice from wise friends and just plain "wise guys." Twinges of guilt and anxiety, while listening to words of unsought advice, are a part of the pain that goes with parenthood of a handicapped child. "Put the poor thing away," say some, "it's not fair to the other children." Others whisper, "How cruel, sending one's own child away to an institution—and such a place."

Truly there is only one solution: ignore everyone, follow your heart and conscience, and do what you think is right.

Little Sue thrived in her new home—counting the nursery of the maternity ward as a home.

"She's just like a rosebud, velvety pink," exclaimed Big Sue.

Little Sue nestled contentedly in the white bassinet. When first we had placed her in a baby bed, she had seemed lost; so we did a quick spray job on the wicker bassinet, bringing it again into service. She was a well-behaved baby—too good—she preferred sleeping to eating. The children idolized her; Todd would sit in his wheelchair beside her, a happy grin on his face, almost unbelieving that a child so tiny could be alive. To Kelly, as she gently caressed the infant's cheek, she was "pretty kitty." To all of us she was a Christmas gift sent from above.

I remember feeling somewhat reproachful for the keen joy this infant brought to our home that Christmas; so unlike the Christmas before with all its illness. I thought also of Susan's parents. It must have been a sad holiday for them.

The usual excitement over gifts was muted, at least for the older girls; they had thoughts only for the baby. Anita, in her final year of high school and planning to enter nursing school in the fall, and already an experienced nurse's aide, hovered over Little Sue like a matron nurse. "Mom, I think she needs to be changed," or "Mom, maybe she should have a new drawsheet, she must have bubbled over." She'd report to me almost every hour, just so she could pick up the baby and hold her.

Often I'd see Suzanne and Helenmarie slipping a hand under the blankets to make sure Susan's diapers weren't wet. During that holiday season, Little Susan was always dry, top and bottom.

One opinion about the baby the children shared unanimously; there was nothing wrong with her, "The dumb doctor made a big mistake." Their father was inclined to agree with them when he said, "She certainly seems normal, eyes and all."

"But it's her heart that has a murmur; and the doctor showed me her palm and explained about the lines on the palm and fingers."

Everyone rushed to look at her hands. "They are just the same as mine," stated Eric, "only smaller."

I shook my head. The doctor was outstanding in his field and never made such a mistake. He had explained to me that there were degrees of mongolism. I said to the children, "Maybe Susie is one of the very mild cases." They reluctantly agreed.

The months passed swiftly. Patches of color on the front lawn surprised us—yellow and lavender crocuses poking their heads through the snow. And as the buds opened, so did little Sue. All winter she was a tiny creature, tightly closed, sleeping and eating, absorbing the warmth and love surrounding her. Gradually, as a delicate flower opens its petals to the embrace of the warm sun, she lifted her head a little higher, her eyes sparkling and smiling all the time.

The days grew longer and warmer. Spring had arrived; so had Robin's sixth birthday.

~ 19 ~
Robin Is Gone

It was spring indoors as well as outdoors. The windows in the kitchen were ablaze with color. The violet blue curtains with wide white fringe appeared more vibrant than ever beside the pots of yellow crocuses and tulips that David had forced to bloom inside.

In October he had planted bulbs of tulip, hyacinth, and crocus in flower pots; these pots he buried deep in the rich loam of his St. Francis garden. It was a small garden under a gnarled old pear tree and near a red brick cabin. The cabin with its steep, slanting roof, which nearly reached the ground, looked quite like an old English cottage.

Seedlings and plants, shielded by the brick wall from the cold winds, flourished. From early April to late autumn, the garden was alive with a march of color: the crocuses, forsythia, tulips, and hyacinths came first; then Japanese iris and poppies, followed by marigolds, zinnias, snapdragons, and phlox in midsummer. The deep-drowsing mums and asters came when the leaves in the trees were aflame.

All this was a boy's tribute to his favorite saint, whose cowled figure stood in a red-roofed shrine fastened to the old pear tree.

In the first week of February, David had dug up the flower pots—a muddy job—and carried them to the fruit cellar in the basement. Here would be enough warmth for the bulbs to sprout—so his favorite teacher, Gert, had taught him.

He was continually asking her about the whys and wherefores of this plant and that tree; from her vast experience in farming and greenhouse culture, she would always come up with explicit answers.

Like Gert, David had a green thumb. The wildflowers he dug up in the woods, no matter how wilted they appeared when he arrived home, he nursed into growth. Anything living, plant or animal, he loved, and the response to his empathy was amazing.

Toni, our dog, usually a sober creature, went into fantastic contortions of affection each afternoon when David descended the steps of the school bus. David's rabbit, a gray Belgian hare, doing nothing but eating all day, hopped after Dave when he hiked into the woods.

Other members of the menagerie were two cats and their perennial kittens, caged hamsters, a field mouse from biology class at school, snakes, an aquarium of fish, and finally Molly, the turtle. She (if not a he) was a gift from David to Todd for Christmas; the motive for this present was not purely altruistic, I suspect. It was rather a good excuse to bring another friend into the house.

The busy, even tenor of our household was upset by a call from Robin's caseworker. She said that the judge of the county probate court had signed commitment papers for Robin's removal to a state institution for the feeble-minded or insane. As soon as a bed was available, he would be taken there.

The unique horror of our visit to the institution, which I had forced into the dark recesses of my memory, emerged again. I felt caught up in a tempest, spun, buffeted, my breath lost in the fetid smells of that school. Lifting Robin from his bed, I held him, trying to draw strength and comfort from him as I had so often in the past—almost six years now. He smelled so sweet and clean; his cheek was smooth and soft against mine.

Lord, why had he lived this long; why must he be stuck in that pen to die? Why can't he stay with us?

Suddenly I recalled a comment of our guide at the state school, "This institution is only one of many in the state, and in some cases the state places children in foster homes."

I set immediately to work, drafting a letter of request to keep Robin. But to whom was I to address it—the governor? the Department of Mental Health? Finally I settled on the social service of the hospital where Robin would be sent for routine evaluation.

Robin had but three weeks left before his scheduled departure. Now it was Bill and I who waited for the mailman. After ten days a letter arrived; it contained a paragraph of bureaucratese, the gist of which was: no, they could do nothing, plus a suggestion that we write to another department, name and address enclosed.

That was a bitter disappointment, but there was still hope. We prayed and dashed off a letter to the address given us. There were only ten days left.

A friend seemed puzzled at our concern. He had no experience of the atmosphere of the state school. Bill said to him, "Whenever a newspaper exposes a case of cruelty to, or neglect of, a dog or cat, the community is outraged. Dorothy and I feel that a child, retarded or normal, should be protected from neglect, as well as an animal. It's that simple. If that is being sentimental, then we're sentimental."

We waited, trying meanwhile to prepare the children for Robin's departure. They spent more time around his bed, winding his music boxes and talking cheerful nonsense, to which he could answer only with a radiant smile.

The daily chores and activities of the youngsters helped distract our minds. When each day's mail brought no answer, we spent the rest of the day with a heavy heart; but by evening, hope renewed our spirits—"Maybe it will be in tomorrow's mail." To a commonsense, practical mind, our behavior would seem odd, irrational; we were always hoping for some miracle—for Todd or Colette, and now for Robin.

April 27 arrived, bright and sunny but with little hope. Today would be Robin's last day. If the mail brought no reply, he would leave early the next morning. Arrangements had been made for an ambulance to take him to the state school. He was too weak to make the long trip by car. What irony, this last concern for him!

The mail arrived. Nothing.

Robin would leave us tomorrow morning. We all suffered that evening.

Morning came too soon. Bill picked at his breakfast and finally pushed it aside, slipped into his coat and hat and went to Robin's room. He patted him and said, "So long, little Robin-bird," and hurried to his car.

The children all wished Robin a weepy good-bye before they dashed out for the school bus.

About 9:00 A.M. the ambulance arrived. I dressed Robin in his little red jacket and cap, kissed him, placed him on the stretcher, and he was gone.

I watched from the window as the long, sleek ambulance sped out of the driveway. Robin was gone. It did not seem real.

I could not understand why Robin couldn't be kept with us; the state hospitals were crowded, and there was a long waiting list. In years to come, over and over, the State Department of Mental Retardation would ask us to keep these children.

I can't remember how long I stood staring out the window, only half seeing the lovely spring unfolding a picture of fresh bright colors under our tall elm trees. Down from a branch flew a robin, he struggled to pull a worm from the moist earth. He was so round, fluffy, brown and red. I watched him as he struggled, and I wept for my Robin-bird.

～ 20 ～
Another Setback

For six years neither snow nor rain nor heat could stay Colette and me from our appointment at the Neurology Clinic every other week. For six years neither the press of household duties, nor sickness nor depression nor any other reason or excuse could keep me from that visit to the specialist; the gleam of hope led me on; the frustrations, and there were many, were minor—not the black kind. Remaining optimistic, I looked back at my daughter's good days when she was free of the clutches of the phantom illness, the still undiagnosed malady. One knew the sun was shining behind the clouds; I was confident Colette would be well some day.

At the present time, however, Colette was going through one of her dark periods. Even as we tried to deny this to ourselves, we were acutely aware of it—and so was Colette. For several months her blackouts continued, as often as forty times a day. The doctor changed her medication frequently, but the hoped-for recovery never came.

Colette was becoming dull and listless, her movements slow and heavy. She seemed like a little girl lost in a dark dream world, trying desperately to reach the forgotten sunshine. The blackouts and the medications were taking their toll.

After one of our long discussions of the pros and cons of her condition, we decided to ask her doctor to take her off drugs to see how she functioned without them. He agreed that we had a point and promised to withdraw the drugs gradually, provided that Colette would be in the hospital. This would be a long-term hospitalization in a convalescent hospital for children.

We began preparing Colette for being away for several months, away at a hospital where the patients went to school (the place had several classrooms).

She was not happy. She felt she did not belong; all the other youngsters were either encased in heavy casts or braces, or seriously ill with heart conditions that kept them confined to their beds.

Colette appeared normal and didn't wake the same response from nurses and others as the helpless ones. She became resentful and uncooperative.

The medications were withdrawn very gradually—one at a time. In what I am sure was an eternity to Colette, three months passed. Still, not all the medications had been discontinued. Colette's blackouts neither increased nor decreased. She continued to fall, and one day had to be taken to emergency to have a head wound stitched. Such episodes made the staff edgy—fearful that irate parents might bring suit for negligence.

Finally, on a cold November morning, I arrived at the hospital in response to the doctor's request for a conference. The trip was treacherous. I fought icy roads and poor visibility in one of our first snowstorms of the winter.

I was tired and tense and should have accepted a cup of hot coffee one of the nurses offered, but I waved it aside with a quick, "No thanks." I wanted to see the doctor and make my visit short, so I could head for home. The weather being what it was, the trip would take a good three hours.

The doctor was grim. He said the staff and he had decided not to withdraw any more medications; it would be too risky. He didn't explain why. Then, the crushing blow, "We think you should send Colette away."

I was stunned. I gasped, "Send her away—where?"

"To the state school," he replied.

My visits to the state hospitals flashed through my mind. I recalled the one large building for teenaged girls, girls Colette's age, who lacked the vitality, color, and excitement that goes with youth. Some stood about in small groups doing nothing; others sat on benches staring listlessly into space; and beyond, the enormous dormitory with its high ceilings, colorless walls, and row after row of beds with barely enough room to walk between. Over all this crowded drabness hung the odor of neglect—of poverty.

I had never pictured my Colette ever being a part of this home, my fears had been for Robin, Michael, and Kelly. Then I remembered another hospital I had visited where we had insisted on being admitted to the maximum security cottage for problem children. *Maximum security*—it had seemed ludicrous to use that term about children.

We were admitted through a barred door to a large circular room, which was poorly lighted and contained a few chairs and a desk. Off this room were several corridors; each was locked off from the circular room by a barred door. Pressed against these cell doors were little children with their arms eagerly outstretched between the bars, begging to be touched—to be loved.

These little ones had small cells along the long corridors. Each cubicle contained a mattress. A few had beds.

The children's corridors seemed to be divided by age. In one corridor sat a tall blond girl talking to an attendant. When I asked why she was there (she appeared normal), I was told she had epilepsy; for that she was in maximum security, confined behind bars. And the little arms reached out begging—how I wanted to take them home—to love, to laughter, to fresh air, to colorful toys and freedom!

This was what this doctor was prescribing for my daughter.

After a long pause to regain my composure, I asked, "Doctor, have you ever been to the state hospital?"

"No."

Precisely and slowly, I suggested, "Before you sentence another child to this incredible place, visit it." As I rose to leave I said I would be taking Colette home. He protested, but was helpless to persuade me to leave her, in the face of his hopeless advice.

After all these years of hope, they were saying she

was hopeless—she was useless, unwanted, better hidden. Get rid of her—a burden to you and society.

I was filled with rage, pity, and love. I gathered Colette and her few belongings and plunged into the storm to drive to the safety and love of our family and home.

~ 21 ~
A New Doctor for Colette

It was a white, cold winter. For the first time in seven years, Colette and I did not make our bimonthly trip to the clinic. We were trying hard to resign ourselves to the thought that Colette's brain was hopelessly and permanently damaged, and nothing could be done to help her.

We had to plan our lives around her illness. This meant being constantly on the alert for her falls. She was never allowed to walk outdoors unless someone was with her. Bike rides, hayrides, and swimming were again forbidden. Indoors, we always settled her in a chair at the table where she was protected from falling. I said, "always," but sometimes we forgot, or she did, and before we were able to reach her, she would fall. Far too often she struck her head and had to be taken to an emergency room for stitches. But one of us tried to have her in view at all times.

Even Todd protested with his typical excited grunts when Colette was in danger.

March 6, Colette celebrated her twelfth birthday. She had grown taller and was lean and lovely, but a sadness had settled into her. She was different, and she was aware of it. How much easier if she had been retarded like Kelly or Little Sue! They hadn't a care in the world and were delightfully happy in their simple carefree world.

I guess no parent of a handicapped child is really ever resigned. We always harbor, deep within our hearts, hope—a strong wish that there is someone, somewhere, or some thing, that can make our children whole. And so as long as Colette's illness did not even have a name—

only brain damage as the doctors always told us—we could not put out the flame of hope.

Spring arrived, the snows giving way to fresh, green sprouts of new life.

One morning a friend, Helen, called. At one time, before her marriage, she had been our baby-sitter. Colette was a baby then, and Helen had a special attachment to her. She had since retained an interest in her. She was excited with news of a new acquaintance whose son had an illness similar to Colette's. He had been taken to the same clinic where we had been taking Colette. Complete failure!

But recently the mother had discovered a doctor in Milwaukee, who now treated her son. His falls were controlled with new medications. He was back in school, attending regular classes, participating in gym and all activities.

I called the woman and heard from her an almost carbon copy of Colette's history. She urged us to write to her doctor.

As the buried seeds of winter sprung into blooming spring, so did the suppressed seed of hope burst into flower again in us. Having had our hopes dashed so many times, we tried to temper our enthusiasm. It would not be easy to arrange the trip if the new doctor would accept Colette as a patient. There were the little ones at home, who would have to have a stay-over babysitter. There was also the expense involved: traveling, hotel, food, doctor bills.

Bill and I sat down and discussed all these problems, trying to weigh them against the odds of any success. But hope and love prevailed. We wrote to the doctor. We asked him to be totally honest with us, because we had no time, money, or heart to waste.

We posted the letter in early May. By the first of June, no answer had arrived. Again we suffered hopelessness. No doubt the doctor felt Colette's case was incurable and didn't bother to write. It hurt us to be ignored. We were resigning ourselves again when a special-delivery letter came.

The doctor apologized for the delay. He had just returned from a month's stay in Europe. Yes, he felt he could help Colette. He set up appointments to see her on June 25, 26, and 27. It would take extensive examination and testing.

What excitement the planning of the trip brought to the household! Helenmarie was about to be graduated from high school, and Anita would be home from nursing school for several weeks' vacation, so they could be our baby-sitters. Our good friend Gert would oversee things during the daytime.

Bill arranged a vacation from work. With our car packed with suitcases (one would think we were going for a month), we set out early in the morning of June 23. Sue came with us to be a companion for Colette.

It had been many years since we had had a vacation; so the trip was festive and full of the joy of hope. We picnicked along the way, where we could relax from the fear of Colette falling, but stopped in the evenings for dinner at restaurants. We became accustomed to the stares as we walked along a street. Bill and I, on either side of Colette, supported her when she blacked out, which now happened over and over and over.

It was easy to talk with the new doctor. He was so human; he seemed to care about all of Colette and all our family.

After a three-hour conference, he instructed us to bring Colette back in the morning, when he would give her an encephalogram and other tests. All would require a great deal of time; so he suggested we go sight-seeing and enjoy ourselves.

When we returned in early afternoon, we found Colette a bit groggy from medication given in the tests. The nurses asked us to be there the next morning for a final talk with the doctor.

We didn't sleep much that night; we were too anxious.

Promptly at 9:00 A.M. we were ushered into the doctor's office. He was cheerful. "To begin with," he said, "I can tell you what's wrong with Colette. She has epilepsy."

For a split second I felt a blow of remembrance—that young girl locked in maximum security at the state hospital. Then I felt relieved that at last I knew.

"The reason it was difficult to diagnose," the doctor

continued, "was because she had several areas of the brain damaged, which gave her several sets of symptoms." He unfolded what appeared, at first, to be a large book. It bore the results of the encephalogram, the written record of Colette's brain activity. He pointed out various spikes which indicated trouble. It was all strange to see, and yet, it was spelled out before us.

"But can you help her?" I begged.

"Yes," he said so firmly that I felt a vast confidence.

He set before us a program for Colette. First was a complete change in medication. Second, we were to set about finding a school for her—preferably a vocational school where she would not have to function under pressure. Third, we were to continue keeping our daily journal and report by letter to him once a week on her progress or any adverse symptoms. We were to return in six weeks for a checkup.

After three hours—how they had flown—our spirits soaring, we left. Never had I felt so certain that Colette would be helped—not cured, as he had explained, but surely controlled, free of her seizures. His positive attitude infected all of us. It was a joyous trip home.

Within two days after Colette received the new medication, the seizures stopped. As the doctors had suggested, she began doing her share of the household chores. She walked about on her own and was happy to be like her sisters and brothers.

It seemed too good to be true. I was apprehensive but chided myself for having little faith.

One week passed, then the explosion! A tremendous crash brought us all rushing to the kitchen. There on the floor writhed Colette, her body twisting and thrashing. This was epilepsy—an epileptic seizure. We had never seen it before, because the drugs she had been taking had prevented her from reaching this pitiful point.

What had we done to her? The guilt feeling was overwhelming. It was hard to face her when she opened her eyes, lying exhausted on the floor.

"Better call the doctor," Bill said, "guess we were wrong again."

It was Saturday. The doctor was playing golf. The secretary would try to get a message to him.

And so we waited. We had put Colette to bed, because as one seizure ended, another took hold. She seemed to be growing weak, and her color had turned bluish.

The hours dragged on. We were approaching the panic stage when the call came.

"This sometimes happens," the doctor said, "but I'd hoped it wouldn't, because Colette had never had a grand mal seizure. Try to be calm. Give me your family doctor's phone number; I'll call him and advise him what to do for Colette. The change in her medication has caused this. Her system has not yet absorbed enough of the new drugs, but when it has, she will be all right. Trust me."

There was no trust left in me; again we had met with failure. We had wasted time and money—and worse, had let Colette down again.

Our family doctor arrived and gave Colette an injection which our new doctor had prescribed to make her sleep.

As we left her room, he counseled us to give it a little more time—not to give up on this new doctor.

There was nothing else to do. And that was the last seizure Colette had.

～ 22 ～
And Todd Makes Seven

It was a June afternoon. I could hear the children shouting as they swam and splashed in the pond.

Bill had just returned from work. I met him at the door. I was in a kind of shock. "The caseworker was here this afternoon. I've been nearly sick since. They're going to take Todd away and put him in the state school for the mentally retarded—like Robin."

Todd! I could hear his voice among the others. With two life jackets carefully adjusted, he could splash about as well as the others.

Todd was seven years old now, still very spastic. He could not speak, sit, or stand unassisted. He had continued to make weekly trips to the Rehabilitation Center for therapy sessions. It was on one of these visits that a county psychologist had given him an I.Q. test. The result accorded with the plans of Child Welfare to place Todd in the state school. We had never thought of this possibility, because Todd was mentally normal.

Through questioning, we learned that the so-called intelligence test given to Todd was a standard test for a normal child of his age group. "How," we asked, "can he answer questions when he can't speak, because of his spastic vocal chords? How can he place blocks when he had no control of his hands? In short, how could any sane, much less, fairminded practitioner of psychometric evaluations claim the results of such a test to be that of this child's intelligence? The most it could prove was that the child was physically unable to participate in such a test."

The answers we received to these objections skirted

the issue. They ranged from blind faith in the instruments of Binet and Wechsler, which excluded any subjective conclusions, to an observation that we were emotionally involved. A psychometric evaluation is presumed to be infallible.

Of course we were emotionally involved! We loved Todd. We were also intelligent enough (we presumed) to observe certain facts and draw reasonable conclusions. Although love is ordinarily called blind, very often love gives deep, revealing insight.

"The mind is far too subtle and complex to be represented by a single score or by only a handful of scores in a test," says Dr. Calvin W. Taylor of the University of Utah. "It is an insult to the human mind to allow this oversimplified view point to survive." How much more does this apply to a handicapped child who is unable to communicate his thoughts!

Thus, we were confronted with the thought that Todd would be placed in the state-school snake pit where the sign over the door should read Abandon All Hope. He would be placed in one of the hundred cribs, which held hopeless and dejected children, and lie for the rest of his life staring at the gray steel girders and filthy windows.

Bill and I knew, with certainty, that Todd would die from a wounded spirit in this place, before dysentery and neglect could do their work.

At this point we heard of a new center where techniques were used to test those who lacked the muscular ability and coordination to take the standard tests. It was called the Mental Development Center and was associated with Western Reserve University.

We then discovered how efficiently meshed were the gears of bureaucracy. We received a letter from the secretary of the psychologist.

Dear Mrs. Gauchat:

We had received a good deal of information in regard to Todd from the Lorain County Health Department and from the Cerebral Palsy and Rehabilitation Center. In going over this material, it seems to us that Todd has been receiving medical care and follow up study. The letter from Mr.———

also indicates that Todd has recently been evaluated by two clinical psychologists, although their findings were not sent to us.

At the present time, we do not feel that we could contribute anything more to the understanding of Todd's condition.

As foster parents, we were helpless, even though we pleaded with Todd's social worker to allow us at least to be present at a testing; so that we could interpret for him. Every appeal fell on deafened ears. In a few months, a deputy sheriff would come into our driveway to take Todd away.

To others, perhaps we appeared foolish in our efforts to help Todd; we were not legally or morally bound to do so. Every day hundreds of children, victims of broken homes (those tragic neo-orphans) suffer a similar fate. Their tragedy is unnoticed, except in a few newspaper columns during the Christmas season, which they share with the neglected, the aged, and homeless derelicts.

According to my conscience, a Christian is morally responsible for his neighbor's well-being in whatever way he is able. "When I was in prison, you visited Me." If only one were able to prevent Christ from being put into prison!

It was then that we grasped the hope of adopting Todd, making him our legal son.

This was no small decision. No one knew better than we did the enormous life responsibility we were taking on. But God seemed to knock down every doubt we had—the biggest one being our responsibility to our own children, especially Colette.

These obstacles were pushed aside when all of our gang heard the idea. And Colette had improved so much under the care of the new doctor; we felt we owed something for that.

As delicately as we could, we suggested adoption to Todd's father. He approved. He had been unemployed for over a year. He told us that Todd had been baptized at the Catholic hospital immediately after birth, when it appeared that he would not live. We called the hospital chaplain, and he verified the baptism from the records.

We became encouraged now that two big obstacles to our adoption were so easily removed.

We consulted an attorney and asked him to represent us in the adoption procedure, which we felt might not be smooth; since we were emotionally involved. After asking us with a searching look whether we fully realized the consequences of the unusual step we were taking, he cheerfully accepted the case for a fee of $100 plus court fees.

In mid-November we were summoned to court—and in a matter of minutes, we signed the papers that made us Todd's legal parents. There was no drama or contest, merely a brief interview with the judge.

We had become parents of a seventh child. Todd Christopher Gauchat was given a formal baptismal ceremony on the Sunday within the Octave of Christmas and was deeply impressed by it.

One of the first things we did as his new parents was to take him to Cleveland Clinic for an I.Q. test. It was given by Miss R., who was noted for her testing of handicapped children. The results were what we had predicted. Todd's I.Q. was normal. We locked this important report in our files along with Todd's birth certificate.

The winter months passed swiftly. Todd reached his eighth birthday March 9. He would now be eligible for a home tutor. I notified the school board. My hope was that Jane E. would be assigned.

Much to our delight, she was. She set about enthusiastically developing a communication system with Todd. He was a real challenge to teach, but Jane, an amazing woman was equal to it. An entire new world was opening to Todd.

In late fall a school psychologist was sent to test him. This was routine, we were told. I was apprehensive but was assured that Jane would be present to interpret for Todd and that the test was geared to his physical handicaps.

We were greatly relieved when he finished. "He did well," the psychologist said. "My report to the state will tell them that this child will profit greatly from school."

Two weeks later he appeared at our door. It was

apparent something serious was wrong. "I'm sorry to have to tell you," he said, "Todd does not qualify for school. I made a mistake on my test. It was brought to my attention at the office."

Anger was furiously building within me. "You know and I know that you didn't make a mistake—your findings simply contradicted the findings of a man who has been testing longer than you—the one who was responsible for all Todd's problems," I told him.

With that I went to my desk and pulled from the files the report from Miss R. "Look at this," I demanded, thrusting the papers into his hands. "There is proof that Todd is mentally normal. Let me make this clear, too. You are now dealing with Todd's mother. If you don't give him a teacher, I will take it to court. I will put you and Lorain County and the machinery of this system that is denying this boy an education in every newspaper in this state."

I was shaking with rage, and the poor young man was speechless.

What he reported to his superiors I will never know, but he must have told them enough to make them reconsider. We never heard from them again. Todd's schooling was never interrupted.

～ 23 ～
A Broken Child

During our trips to the state hospital, we had never envisioned Colette or Todd ever being a resident of one of them. Both had handicaps, but neither was retarded. The fact that children like them were locked behind bars added another dimension of horror to our thinking.

Colette and Todd were forever safe with us, but we did have to brace ourselves for the exodus of Kelly and Michael, nearing their sixth birthdays.

Kelly was still the teasing little imp; and Michael, still only the size of a three-year-old, remained the silent, independent one, often lost in his private world.

First came word that Kelly was to be transferred. It was an aching, tearful departure, even though it had a humorous side.

A uniformed officer from the sheriff's department arrived early one morning. He had an assistant with him, in case the patient became unmanageable (violent was another way of saying it). Kelly was her charming, beautiful self. Her blue eyes sparkled, and her golden curls bobbed as she stretched out her arms to greet these ill-at-ease serious gentlemen.

"Hi, Cookie," she chirped, her arms outstretched, waiting to be lifted by one of them from her wheelchair. The officer appeared flustered and awkward as he lifted her in his arms. It was a picture of contrasts; the uniformed officer, with gun in holster dangling from his side, carrying curly-headed Kelly to the waiting, official car.

Just that swiftly, she was gone. There are no words to describe the tearing of the heart.

Months later, Michael was taken away, too. In the meantime Kelly's bed had been taken by two-year-old Kenny, another beautiful, curly-headed redhead. He was as fragile as Kelly was healthy.

Kelly was strong. To a degree, she would be able to fend for herself. It was another matter with Michael. He was small and delicate. A child of the same age would be able to overpower him, as Kelly had done on several occasions, stripping him to the skin.

I feared what might happen to him if he were placed in that barn-like cottage, where a hundred children were locked in one room to roam around with nothing to do. Would he be allowed to have his two small toys, or would they be snatched away?

Michael's mother went to visit him monthly. She was a widow, who had to support him and his twin sister. Because she had to work, she could not care for him at home. Her visits were anguish for her. She would weep as she recalled the day's events and the condition in which she found Michael. She always provided adequate and attractive clothing for him, but often she would find him in oversized old clothing and without shoes or with shoes that did not fit or even match. This was his apparel in wintertime; in summer he had only a diaper; or more often, he and the other children were naked.

Michael's mother was a timid woman who never complained. Many times she found Michael with his head shaved where stitches had been sewn to close a wound, no doubt inflicted by the rough behavior of some of the larger boys. When I suggested that she enter a complaint to the superindendent, she always gave the excuse that a complaint might anger the staff, who in turn might take out their feelings on Michael.

Robin and Kelly later were moved out of that school, but Michael was destined to die there.

The children were busy with Christmas preparations when Michael's mother stopped on her way to work.

"I have a favor to ask," she said. "I would like to bring Michael home for Christmas. Would you care for him during the day? I can't take off from work because the holiday season is a busy time at work." (She was a waitress.)

"Of course, we'd be glad to have him back," was our instant response.

We were shocked to see how thin he had become. His once curly dark hair was clipped short, and two areas of his head were shaved, exposing the stitched wounds of falls or blows. And he was hungry. He ate like a starved animal, gulping and slopping his food, hardly taking time to catch his breath.

He spent the holidays with us by day and returned home each evening with his mother. The day before New Year's Eve, he returned to the state school. It was dreadfully hard to see him return to his inhuman existence.

New Year's Eve the phone rang. Michael's mother sobbed, "Michael has had a serious accident. He is undergoing brain surgery. Could you come?"

"I'm on my way," I replied.

I explained to Bill, scrambled into my coat, and departed.

I found Michael's mother near hysteria. Her aunt, who had been summoned, was trying to calm her. Little Ann, Michael's twin, crouched in a big chair, looking terrified.

The story, as I pieced it together, was that Michael had received a severe blow to his head and had been taken to a hospital in the city. There was a chance the doctors could save his life with immediate surgery. His mother had been asked to authorize it.

Time had been precious. The doctors could not wait for her to go to the city and sign consent papers. By phone she had given permission to operate, but was given no information about the accident.

"Would you call for me?" she asked.

I placed a call to the hospital, but could get no information. "Please, God," I prayed, "help her to get hold of herself for Michael's sake and little Ann."

I cannot remember what I said to her, but gradually she calmed. The only thing to do was to go to the hospital. We could be with Michael and talk to the doctors personally.

Michael suvived the surgery, but our Hummingbird was forever grounded. He never regained consciousness.

He lay in a coma, paralyzed and sightless, for the rest of his life—two full years.

He remained in the city hospital for several weeks and then was transferred back to the state school to one of the bed wards close to the so-called hospital wing. I visited him there—this tragic victim of our do-nothingness. We, citizens of this rich state, have done nothing for our broken children. We have done nothing about providing funds to hire enough staff to watch over, love, and protect them. We have done nothing to provide funds for decent equipment for their barnlike home—not even screens on the windows to keep the flies and other insects out of the sores of these helpless victims.

It made me ill to see Michael lying motionless, unseeing, unfeeling—this little Michael whose joy had been to flit about like a bird.

His mother never knew for certain how the accident had occurred. One person said he'd fallen, another that he had been pushed, another that an older child had picked him up and thrown him against a wall.

I pleaded with his mother to give the story to the newspapers, not only for Michael's sake but for the sake of all the children locked behind those walls. If the public would know, pressure could be brought to get more funds to improve these unspeakable conditions.

But to the end, she refused, fearful that any complaint might bring more harm to Michael. Indeed, she could find only words of praise for the staff at the hospital, and she was certainly correct about that. They were dedicated people, working under horrible conditions, trying to do an impossibly big job. There were just not enough of them.

On Christmas Eve, two years almost to the day after his injury, Michael died.

～ 24 ～
The Fantasy Turned Nightmare

The July sun beat down on the blue waters of Lake Erie. Even at 8:30 in the morning, the day was warm—by noon it would be hot. The parking lot, which could be seen from the boat, was filling up, each car spilling out passengers and picnic gear. Crowds were moving up the gangplank; a festive air was spreading through the ship.

Laughter was contagious; everyone was caught up in the excitement of the fun hours ahead aboard the pleasure boat that sailed between Cleveland and Detroit—one day to Detroit, next day back to Cleveland.

Colette and I were making the trip to Milwaukee for her three-month checkup. We had decided to combine pleasure with business. We would visit friends in Detroit, then take off for Milwaukee by plane.

The boat was one of the largest pleasure boats sailing the Great Lakes. It had restaurants, a swimming pool, a dance floor, and a theatre; plus spacious lounges indoors. Great areas of deck space, filled with comfortable deck chairs, permitted hours of soaking up the sun and the lake breezes.

We settled ourselves in chairs. But Colette was not content to sit. She wanted to explore. I took her on her first tour, but she rapidly learned the layout and spent much of the morning wandering from deck to deck.

It was the strangest feeling to watch her walk about alone; we had been so used to watching every move she made. We had so much to thank God for. Yet there were times when her behaviour troubled us, too.

Our Detroit friend met us at the dock and drove us to his home in the country, where we had a happy reunion with his family. (Their youngest son, Brian, had suffered severe brain damage from an infancy infection. He reminded me of Robin in his helplessness.) After dinner the girls took Colette outdoors to see their horse and the other farm animals. Their father offered to take me to visit a school for exceptional children, conducted by a religious order of nuns.

Since our first visit to Milwaukee, we had been hunting, unsuccessfully, for a school which would meet Colette's needs. Discouraged, we had enrolled her at our parish school, where her sister-teacher tried hard to work with her. It was frustrating for both.

The visit to the Detroit school was unsuccessful, too. The sister, who received Lou and me, said Colette was too old for their program; she was fourteen, and twelve was the age limit.

Next morning I was tired; Colette wasn't. At dawn I was awakened by her talking, not to me but to herself or some creature of her imagination. This had bothered me for some time, as I had told the doctors when we were still going to the clinic. They seemed unconcerned about it and wrote me off as a worrisome parent when I voiced my fears of her becoming a crippled personality.

When we arrived in Milwaukee, I explained my fears to our new doctor. He seemed convinced that Colette would outgrow these childish fantasies.

He was pleased with her recovery from seizures. His chief concern was to find a school for Colette, one where she would find fulfillment without pressure. He urged us to continue searching.

Another appointment was set. We left feeling encouraged and grateful.

Several weeks later, reading a newspaper, I noticed an item announcing the opening of a school for exceptional children to be operated by the Sisters of St. Joseph. I flew to the telephone; the paper said only twelve children would be accepted.

The sister in charge said she was sure Colette would fit into the program.

Driving home after the first class, Colette couldn't tell me fast enough what went on. Then her face clouded.

"Why was there a mongoloid in the school?" she asked. "This isn't a school for the retarded."

I explained that the school was for brain-damaged children, and in a way a mongoloid is damaged. The explanation seemed to satisfy her; the sunshine came back into her face. But the worry about being retarded still weighed on her mind. As the weeks passed, she reminded us again and again that she was not retarded. Repeatedly we assured her she wasn't and reexplained the reasons for Our Lady of Angels School.

One day I found Colette behind the little brick cabin back of our house, weeping pitifully, and crying over and over, "I'm not retarded." What we had thought to be a dream come true was turning into a nightmare.

Summer classes ended. We thought the short vacation before classes resumed would give Colette a chance to rest and forget her worry. At times she seemed to do that; she was gay and excited when she told her friends about her school. Then suddenly, she would sink into silent depression. This went on for several weeks.

One day, Colette didn't come in for lunch. I found her curled up on the lawn, staring into space. She looked at me as if she didn't know me.

"Time for lunch, Colette—come in—everyone is waiting for you."

It was no use; she seemed rooted to the earth. Her face was shrouded in utter misery. I reached to try to bring her to her feet, but she refused to move or to speak. In that instant I knew (as once before I had known) that Colette was gravely ill.

Racing to the house, I asked Bill to come quickly. He, too, tried to talk to Colette, but it was as if he were talking to a statue.

I phoned the doctor in Milwaukee. Quietly he said, "Colette seems to be suffering from a mental breakdown. You could bring her here, but I would have to hospitalize her, and that might not prove practical for you. Let me call your family doctor, and we will decide what course to take."

Time dragged as we awaited word. I made lunch and set it before Colette. She left it untouched. Bill and I were helpless—terrified—filled with a sinking sickness beyond description. Finally, our family doctor called and said he had arranged for a neuropsychiatrist to see Colette. We were to bring her to University Hospital.

She refused to move, and the doctor had to come and give her an injection to put her to sleep.

This period in our lives was a haze of mental torture, fears, long visits to the hospital, kindly nurses and staff, who cared for strangely ill and broken human beings, and through it all, the hopeless feeling that Colette was lost to us forever. For weeks Colette did not recognize us. She was living in a world of fantasy, speaking only to strange make-believe people, hearing voices that no one else heard. I remembered her conversations with make-believe friends when I had shared her room at our friends' home. I remembered my intuitive concern when I complained to the doctors about my fears of her having a crippled personality. The family was enveloped in a heavy sadness. I found myself weeping until my eyes and head ached.

Added to this suffering was an overwhelming feeling of guilt. Guilt, because we had taken the extra children and guilt for every impatient act, word, or thought that I had had about Colette, dating back as far as my pregnancy with her.

We had long talks with our doctors about her and how her illness affected us and our family. Perhaps I was becoming irrational, blaming myself for taking the extra children. Our family doctor knew us and the family situation. He tried to assure us that the children had nothing to do with this breakdown; it had been building up for years in ways that even the medical men could not explain. There was so little known about the causes of such an illness.

The doctor said that caring for the other children was a form of therapy for me, which helped us to bear Colette's long illness. His words brought me no comfort; all I wanted was to bring Colette home, well, and care for her and keep her healthy.

I made up my mind to give up the foster children. Bill left the decision to me. Making up my mind and carrying out my decision were two different matters.

When I'd return from the hospital and the children

swarmed about me vying for attention, I melted in their love and needs. Baby Susan, the little mongoloid, was an enchanting little ham, who was constantly putting on a show for all of us. The life of this beautiful, adorable baby was a subject, years later, of in-depth discussion at one of the Joseph Kennedy, Jr. awards conferences. The thought that parents and professionals had actually allowed a mongoloid baby to starve to death because the parents couldn't see her worth as a human being was beyond our comprehension, then and now.

To give up the children seemed entirely and utterly impossible; but each day when we visited Colette—and even though, after several months, she was improving—I would resolve to call the agency or parents and give them up.

Finally we did give up Tommy, but he was the only one of the five. It seemed that God had stayed our hand: he had his plans for these children.

At the hospital Colette improved slowly. She recognized us again, but her thinking processes were still disorganized; her fantasies mingled with realities.

At home, we pulled ourselves together. The oppressive sadness and despair left us. We were again filled with hope.

~ 25 ~
The Transformation of Todd

Colette's illness ravaged the entire family—especially Todd. Sue and Helenmarie were in New York City; they had saved their baby-sitting earnings to finance a holiday. When we met them at the bus station on their return, we postponed telling them the bad news until we arrived at home. They were stunned.

Of all the children, Todd seemed to be suffering the most. He was silent, downcast. Often, I noticed a haunted look in his eyes. It was doubly hard for him, because he could not speak—how horribly frustrating not to be able to unburden one's thoughts.

One day as I lifted him from his wheelchair, I staggered slightly under his weight. His limbs jerked for fear I would drop him. I held him closely. He had grown so much. With the weight of his steel braces, which reached from toes to chin, he would soon be too much for me to handle.

He seemed to want me to talk to him. I put him on the floor and curled up beside him. "Something bugging you?" I asked.

He nodded.

"About Colette?"

Yes and no, came the jerking replies.

"More than Colette?"

Again he nodded. I had to stab in the dark with questions to root out his trouble.

"I know you feel bad about Colette, but this had nothing to do with you. Are you blaming yourself?"

He hesitated; he couldn't make me understand. Finally I managed to interpret from him that he was afraid

134

we wouldn't want to keep him. He blamed himself to a degree for Colette's illness and worried that we had regrets about adopting him. He felt he was such an added burden to us; it upset him when I was sad.

How incredibly frustrating for him to have all this caged within him. Suddenly I felt ashamed for allowing myself to be so full of self-pity that the entire family had sunk into a despairing state. We were not helping Colette this way. We could not allow her suffering to destroy the entire family.

I looked at Todd with gratitude. "No matter what happens, Todd, you are our son forever," I assured him. "We're not sorry we adopted you; you are so special to us; you'll never know how much you've done for me."

Indeed, he'll never know how much he's done for countless others. He is an inspiration to everyone. One dared not continue wallowing in self-pity when one had good health, strong body, working limbs, a voice that could form words. Todd had none of these, but he had a deep and perceptive mind aware of the feelings of others and of the wonders of creation surrounding him. He had a heart full to overflowing with love and generosity—a sense of humor about everything—mostly himself.

When he implied he wanted to help he meant it. This set me to thinking again about something that had been bothering me for months. I had begun to question the value of his braces. He had been going to therapy for seven years now, and there was little, if any, improvement in his attempts at walking. He could not control his legs and arms at the same time. It seemed clear to me that he would never walk; all that the braces were doing was keeping him sitting straight as a soldier. Was it worthwhile encasing him in steel which prevented him from rolling about on the floor and perhaps learning to do things with his hands?

As I sat beside him on the floor, I told him of my feelings. He looked at me intently, thinking, maybe for the first time, about this possibility. And as I have so often done since, I tossed the problem in his lap.

"You're the only one who knows how it feels to have

cerebral palsy. I don't. What do you think about hanging up the braces for a while?''

All sorts of possibilities surfaced.''Maybe you could learn to dress yourself, and maybe you could take care of your toilet needs. You know the braces are so heavy I won't be able to lift you on the toilet much longer.''

His eyes flashed with the excitement of a new challenge. He was ready to begin.

''Tonight,'' I said, ''we'll start after dinner. You're to try to undress and maybe even put on your own pajamas. Just remember one thing—this much I know about cerebral palsy—you must relax. Make yourself feel like an old rag doll, and then I think you'll have some control over your hands.''

He was ecstatic. All those dark clouds of the past days were dispelled. He had known so much insecurity in his short life but was secure again.

That evening I tossed his pajamas on the living room floor and took off his braces (he was never to wear them again). ''You wanted to help, go to work and see if you can figure out how to undress yourself and put on those pajamas.''

I left him and went to feed Susan. Helenmarie popped into the room, scolding me. ''Mom, you can't make him do it—he can't—have a heart! He's rubbing his elbows raw on the carpeting trying to undress.''

She'll never know how guilty I felt, but I had enough faith in Todd to know that he'd keep on trying for a good long time before he gave up.

An hour elapsed. I looked in on him. By this time, the rest of the children were standing around, wanting to help, but he shook off their attempts. He would succeed.

I smiled to myself, because in that moment I knew he would.

Two hours went by. Todd was soaked in perspiration, but he had undressed himself and put on his pajamas. He was triumphant!

Gradually, he sped up the process. It was amazing. If I was in another room, I could hear him sighing, drawing in deep breaths so he could relax. It was in these moments of relaxation that he had some control over his hands. From that day on, he dressed and undressed himself, except for putting on his high-laced shoes.

Dressing was not Todd's only achievement. One day I heard him rolling on the floor. Then the plastic urinal banged against the tile floor, and I knew he had met his own toilet need. He was so proud!

Todd's successes brought joy and pride to the family and cleared away all doubt that the children should remain with us. In his studies Todd continued to make progress, but there were times when I am sure his teacher wished that he could speak. He read well (especially the sports pages of the daily paper). He could be tested with multiple-choice examinations, in which a nod of his head would indicate his answer.

He was in third grade when we toyed with the idea of getting him a typewriter. It would have to be an electric one, which needed only a light touch.

Bill had his doubts. "An uncontrolled thrust of his hand could wreck the delicate machine."

But Bill had his secret hopes for Todd. One day he visited an office equipment store. He explained Todd's condition. The clerk summoned a service man. Among the three of them, they came up with the idea to make a plate with finger holes for over the keys. Todd would learn to get his finger into the correct hole.

The price dashed our enthusiasm—$500. We couldn't possibly afford it. But Todd was meant to have a typewriter. When we mentioned the matter to his godmother, she said, "Get it. Send me the bill."

Bill built a desk in Todd's classroom, complete with overhead shelves to hold his books, papers, and such boyish treasures as autographed baseballs. The typewriter was bolted to the desk.

Todd was so excited that he was more spastic than usual. "Relax. Remember, you're an old rag doll," I crooned, trying to quiet him.

I studied the situation. It was apparent that Todd couldn't concentrate on using one finger of one hand and, at the same time, hold the other hand still. He was left-handed, so I tied his right hand to his wheelchair.

Next were the fingers. When he tried to use the index finger, the other four spread out and got in the way. This was solved with an old kid glove. I cut off the index finger, put his hand in it, and bound the other curled-up fingers.

Then I sat down for one of our talks.

"If I have said it once, Todd, I've said it a million times. I don't know what it feels like to be spastic, and besides, I don't know a thing about typing. Only you know how it feels, so you are going to have to figure this out all by yourself. All I ask is that before you try, take a deep breath and relax. Feel like an old rag doll!" With that I left him.

Bill was aghast when he heard what I had done. "He'll wreck the machine," he groaned.

I must confess that I had moments of doubt.

Then suddenly we heard Todd's laughter. We dashed in. He was beaming with pride and dripping with sweat.

Across the top of the page, neatly typed, was TODD CHRISTOPHER GAUCHAT.

~ 26 ~
Bill's Time Has Come

Colette never fully recovered. In a way her thinking process was as uncoordinated as Todd's muscle and nerve control. There were times when she was lucid; at other times she lived in a world of fantasy.

She spent her days knitting, reading (she no longer had any recall of what she read), painting, and praying. She had a deep devotion to the Virgin Mary, and often we found her on her knees in her bedroom, or curled up on her bed reading from her worn-out First Communion prayer book.

The doctor was uncertain about her complete recovery but continued to hope for it. We no longer made plans for her future. We took each day as it dawned. Occasionally she spoke about Our Lady of the Angels School. She never seemed to want to go back, and we were satisfied to have her at home, safe with us, under no pressures, and reasonably happy.

It was not easy to listen to her when she spoke the utter nonsense of her fantasy world. But this other world did have its humorous aspects. And we were such a busy family that not much time was wasted on self-pity or unreasonable hope.

Still, to say we got over Colette's illness would be untrue. There were nights when I cried myself to sleep. I don't think the wound of having a handicapped child ever heals completely.

Todd grew more independent each day. He taught himself to get in and out of his wheelchair, and in and out of bed. School and sports were his joys, and his days were full—busy with books, typewriter, and watching sports on television.

Bill devised a talking board, which had the alphabet painted on it in the same order as the keys on the typewriter. With this, Todd could hold conversations with all of us, spelling out the words. This took a painfully long time, but we learned to abbreviate words, or to catch his thoughts before he completed sentences.

Todd was pure joy. It was exciting to watch his progress and determination. He wanted to complete his independence by learning how to feed himself, but his attempts landed food in his lap or on the floor.

At this point, we turned to professionals for help. We enrolled Todd in Rose Mary Center, a residential facility for handicapped children in Cleveland. With their skilled professional staff, we hoped he would be able to achieve his new ambition.

It was a new experience for Todd, being away from home for the first time. But it was an enriching time of meeting new friends and adjusting to all kinds of unfamiliar situations.

After six months of intensive training, the therapists agreed that Todd would never be able to feed himself or have a normal speech pattern. I can't say we were surprised by this prognosis; he had already achieved far more than any professional had expected.

Our family was growing and moving on, too. Anita was now married. Helenmarie, a college graduate, was a member of the Peace Corps in El Salvador, Central America. Sue was away in college, Eric in high school, and David, involved in gardening, painting, and caring for his menagerie, did as little studying as he could get away with.

Since Robin, Kelly, and Michael had been taken from us, we had had a steady flow of children to fill their beds. Some, like Kim, returned to their families; others died.

Little Sue, who as an infant had reminded me of a pink rose bud, which slowly unfolded its petals, was no longer the quiet one. She had turned into the mischievous imp, searching out ways to tease the older children. Red-headed Joey, who had come to us at the age of two months, was a mischief maker, too. He was fond of rounding up shoes, blankets, toys, towels, and tooth brushes and throwing them into the clothes chute.

Curly-haired blond Mary joined the family when she was three. She had pixie-like eyes which made one feel she was always looking into a never-never land.

She and Sue were inseparable. They were good together or naughty together; and if they were in the play yard together and suddenly disappeared, you could be sure they were sitting in the cherry tree—together. They were about the same size, shared the same room, and loved it when I bought them the same style shoes.

Silvery-haired Steven surprised everyone with his slow but steady progress. He was brought to us at age two with the prognosis of being a bed patient for the rest of his life. He had many problems, besides being retarded; the major one being that he was almost blind. He learned to feed himself after years of painstaking effort, to walk haltingly (like a woundup toy soldier), and finally to master the toilet.

Finally, there was Tim, who was deaf and blind—and stubborn. Had he not been blind and deaf, nothing would have kept him in one place. He was a happy, energetic boy.

The trouble with children is that they grow. It would have been convenient to keep them one size; we were all rather comfortable in the early infancy stage. Our fifteen-room home was full but not crowded.

But they grew. Soon they left playpens and crawled about all the rooms, until that became hazardous for everyone. Then a large bedroom upstairs was converted into a playroom, complete with screen door so they could hear and watch the older kids. The walls were decorated with murals of Charlie Brown and his friends, painted by David.

It wouldn't be long before Susie and Mary would have to leave their cribs for larger beds. Todd was hemmed in with Joey sharing his room. I found myself making mental drawings of an addition to our home, with a large room for Todd and a shower with a faucet close to the floor so he could take his own baths.

Bill did not share my enthusiasm when I mentioned

the idea. Perhaps I caught him at the wrong time—lately he seemed to tire easily. Or, I reasoned, he couldn't appreciate the problem because he was away from it all day. He worked such long hours, traveling to Cleveland every morning, leaving at 6:30 and not returning until 6 in the evening.

I waited for a good moment to broach the subject again. But every time, his reply was emphatic. "Let's make do with what we have."

I knew that once Bill's mind was made up, it was hard to change; but this time he seemed unreasonable to me. Again, I blamed his apparent fatigue. His vacation was coming, and this would be a specially exciting one. I felt that a good rest could change his mind, plus the prayers the little ones sent heavenward every evening.

Passing by, one could hear Mary and Sue "ordering," "Please give us a new house, do you hear, God!"

We were going to celebrate our wedding anniversary. Anita and her husband, Dick, bought us round-trip tickets to El Salvador to visit Helenmarie. And they volunteered to move in to take care of the children while we were gone.

It was too good to be true. We, who had never traveled beyond the East Coast, would be visiting a strange country, thousands of miles from Avon, Ohio.

The weeks before our departure were wildly exciting. Travel arrangements had to be made—passports, immunization, wardrobe. The latter proved the most difficult. Helenmarie had written that we should bring enough clothing for frequent changes, because the weather would be extremely hot and humid.

Time swept by swiftly. Our departure was one week off. Bill had arranged his vacation to allow a few days off prior to departure to get rested and packed.

The last day of work, he arrived home exhausted. His color was ashen.

"I think you should see the doctor before we leave," I suggested. The next day he did.

I was outdoors with the children, who were scampering about in the dry leaves, when Bill returned. It was a warm, golden fall day.

"Well, did you get a tonic?" I asked.

"No, the doctor wants to have X-rays and blood work done tomorrow at the hospital," he answered.

"Hey, this sounds serious."

"Probably nothing that sun and rest won't cure," he replied.

I was packing and repacking suitcases when Bill returned from his examinations. "Well, what's the diagnosis?" I asked, almost cheerfully.

Bill was silent. I looked up from my work and met his eyes. "He wants to see you; says I have something showing in my lungs, and the blood tests indicate tumors somewhere in my body."

I dropped into the nearest chair, disbelieving. Bill continued, "He wanted to put me in the hospital immediately."

The house was unusually quiet that evening; the bustling preparations were set aside. The stillness was broken by the ring of the telephone. A doctor in the Peace Corps headquarters in Washington was speaking. "We are sorry to tell you that we have received word from our office in El Salvador that your daughter, Helenmarie, has been hospitalized with hepatitis." The voice continued, "We do not want you to be alarmed, but it can be serious, and we wanted you to know that she is being given the best care possible. We will keep you informed."

What was God trying to do to us? Two such dreadful announcements in one day! We were frantic with concern for Helenmarie, away in a strange country.

"One thing is sure," Bill said emphatically, "we are going on our trip as planned. We've got to see her."

The next day I kept my appointment with the doctor. "I believe your husband has multiple myeloma," he said gently.

"What is that?"

"It's cancer of the bone."

Then he inquired, "How important is this vacation to you? I would like Bill to go the hospital immediately."

"How long does he have?" Somehow I got the words out.

"No one can be sure, but I would say from three to six months," he replied.

I was shocked, confused, adding and subtracting

months. If the doctor was right, Helenmarie might never see her father again; she had a year to go in the Peace Corps.

Finally I said, "If he is as sick as you say, and has only a short time to live, I can't see that postponing the hospital two weeks will make any difference. To me it's more important that he see our daughter, who is seriously ill herself."

He agreed, and gave me prescriptions for medicine which would help Bill during the trip.

How can I describe my feelings when, with one stroke of the hand of God, my entire life, past and future, seemed to disintegrate?

I took a roundabout way home. I found myself feeling guilty. Bill had been so tired! I felt ashamed that I had nagged him about adding to the house.

The house—suddenly it dawned on me; there would be no need for extra room, for surely the foster children would have to leave now. And what of our children who were still at home with us? What of Colette and Todd?

I was overwhelmed. Tears streamed down my face.

"We've got to take our lives a day at a time," I told myself at last.

"We've got to remain calm and put on a strong front for the children's sake. Above all, we must pray; God will see us through."

By the time I got home, I felt a bit more at peace.

That evening, Bill and I agreed that we would put this nightmare out of our minds and for the next two weeks enjoy every precious moment we had together.

~ 27 ~
A Gift from Guadalupe

The air was cold and crisp the morning of our departure for El Salvador. As the plane climbed, we broke through the clouds into brilliant sunshine.

It was dark when we touched down in San Salvador. Helenmarie had written that Peace Corps volunteers would meet us. A group of young men and women approached, carrying armloads of flowers. With them was a priest. He put out his hand and said, "Welcome! I'm Father Tom Sebian, missionary from your daughter's diocese. I promised Helenmarie I'd bring you directly to the hospital."

Helenmarie, he told us, was recovering. We told him what had happened to us in the past week. We did not want to tell Helenmarie, but the time would come when she would have to know. Father Tom promised to break the news to her when the doctors thought she was strong enough.

We expected to find Helenmarie looking jaundiced, but she was as lovely as ever, fair of skin, her blond hair spread over the pillow. It was a happy, tearful reunion.

"Daddy, you're so pale. Was the trip too much?"

"It was a long trip. I'll get a lot of rest and sunshine while we're here," he replied.

The following day was a relaxed and restful one, spent with Helenmarie, catching up on the latest news. There was a steady stream of visitors to see her.

Father Tom suggested that we join him at his mission parish in La Union for the weekend. It was agreed, and Helenmarie was happy to know we'd be seeing the country and its people, whom she loved.

Running north and south through El Salvador is the two-lane International American Highway, winding up, down, and around the mountains. It is shared with pedestrians, mule-drawn carts, and herds of oxen.

It was an exhausting trip, filled with tension and fears. Father Tom took it all casually, blasting his horn as he went around curves.

I shall never forget the beauty of the exquisite tropical flower the bougainvillea, which grew bountifully along the roadsides.

La Union is a port on the Pacific Ocean, dotted with multicolored houses with bright red orange tile roofs. The church and the town square are the heart of the little city.

The heat was almost unbearable when we reached the mission compound. By evening the air was cooled by a torrential downpour that interrupted electrical service for more than a day.

The hospitality shown us by Father Tom and his co-workers Father Denis and Father Bill was heartwarming.

The next morning we went with Father Denis; he offered mass at a penitentiary nearby. The altar was an old table in the prison courtyard. Prisoners, young and old, male and female—the latter surrounded by their children, some nursing their babies—strolled or squatted in clusters. They were supervised by rifle-bearing guards. All were poor, barefoot, and ragged, but they greeted Father Denis eagerly and joined in fervent prayer as he brought Christ to them in the consecration of the bread and wine.

Next morning we were awakened by firecrackers, cymbals, and drums. It was 6:00 A.M. Outdoors, a procession was in progress. It was led by a band, followed by worshippers and men carrying a colorful statue honoring St. Ludmilla, whose feast was celebrated that day. We learned that this kind of festivity was almost a daily occurrence with these deeply religious people.

We had promised not to talk about Bill's illness, but the promise was difficult to keep when I saw his exhausted, pale face. Father Tom suggested that he rest in the afternoon, and he invited me to travel with him by jeep on his parish rounds.

We went through a jungle and up the side of a volcano to a little village of very poor farmers. As we drove by thatch-roofed huts, it was difficult to believe we were living in the twentieth century. Homes were single rooms, with a hammock stretched across the entire hut. Flour was ground between stones; cornmeal bread was baked in outdoor ovens.

Here, on the volcano, Father Tom, his co-workers, and his parishioners were restoring a four-hundred-year-old church. It was obvious their work had only begun, for old furniture and benches were stored at the rear of the edifice. There was no altar, and Father Tom improvised one on a bench.

As he removed spotless mass linens from a small suitcase, the congregation assembled slowly. Unlike the people in the city of La Union, these peasants were colorless—drab and ragged in their poverty. Their attention was centered on the priest; their eyes never left him as he offered the Holy Sacrifice. The church was silent, save for the coughing of a sick child and a strange flapping sound. There were no lights except two glowing tapers. The ceiling was high, vaulted, and dark.

After mass Father Tom visited briefly with his people and introduced me to some of them. They bowed shyly. Then we set off for the mission, which he wanted to reach before dark.

"What was that flapping sound I heard in the church?" I asked Father Tom.

"That," he laughed, "was hundreds of bats that have made the cathedral their home. We'll have to find an exterminating company to rid the place of them before we complete the renovation."

I was glad he hadn't told me this before mass; I would not have set foot inside had I known.

As much as we enjoyed our stay with the missionaries, we were anxious to return to San Salvador to be with our daughter.

The following week was a busy one. Each day's events had been planned by Helenmarie and her friends to fill every precious moment, introducing us to the friendly people of this tropical country.

Helenmarie lived in a barrio, a small town called San

Antonia Abod, in the jungle. The immense trees, vines, and flowers, made lush by the daily downpours, kept the air moist and humid.

Her barrio people welcomed us with bouquets of jasmine and roses, fireworks, dancing, and special fancy foods made only on great occasions. We were deeply moved by this outpouring of love for us, strangers from far away, and knew it was because our daughter had grown into their hearts.

One of Helenmarie's jobs in the Peace Corps was teaching a class of retarded and emotionally disturbed children. We spent a morning in her school getting to know her pupils, meeting the other teachers, and observing their amazingly progressive methods.

Because of Helenmarie's work with the handicapped, we were introduced to Dr. Ching. He was the head of the Mental Health Department, and a professor at the medical school. He also was responsible for the Rehabilitation Center, which had recently opened; indeed, a wing of it was still under construction.

Children were brought in by bus or car for treatment by doctors, nurses, and therapists imported from Holland, England, and Argentina. They not only worked with the children, but trained native personnel to follow through after they left.

Dr. Ching invited us to join in a group-therapy session which he conducted with the mothers of the handicapped children under treatment at the center. Of course everything was in Spanish, but we could sense the suffering these mothers were undergoing because of their children. In introducing us, he told them something of our background, and mentioned that we had two handicapped children of our own.

One little woman, who seemed particularly distraught, directed a question to me. Dr. Ching translated for me, but first told me about her. She was very poor; her husband had deserted her; she had a hyperactive and retarded little boy, who had to be watched constantly. She was at the breaking point, and she was frightened and needed help.

Her question was, "Do you ever feel like killing your child?"

Her question pierced my innermost feelings. For the first time, I revealed my deep fears. "I have never wanted to kill my Colette, but I pray daily that she dies before I do; so that she will always have me to protect her."

Trying to help her, I suggested that she make a gate to block off one room, where her son could play alone. Before I could finish, I remembered the one-room shacks and thatched huts. To this woman, two rooms would have been a luxury. I often think of her and pray that a way can be found to help her.

Dr. Ching asked me to join him in a class with his medical students who would be touring the mental hospital. Bill remained behind, visiting with Helenmarie. It was a shocking experience, but not nearly as shocking as my visits to our state hospitals at home.

The buildings were ancient and sparsely furnished. There were a few private rooms with beds and bed linen, but most of the population was housed in big dormitories—one for the males, the other for the females. Both dormitories had children in them.

It was mid-afternoon, and the buildings were empty because all the patients were outdoors. The women and girls were in an open compound guarded by women attendants. A few were busy doing handwork, and some were hanging laundry on the walls to dry in the hot sun.

The prevailing feeling was one of sadness. One woman approached me, weeping, begging for something. I could not understand. I reached out and stroked her cheek, much to the dismay of one of the students who feared that she might hurt me.

The men's enclosure was shocking. Here, hundreds of men stood milling about or curled up on the stone floor. All were naked. They were silent; they ignored our presence.

When an attendant appeared with a tray of medication, there was instant response from the patients, who reached out for their pills—tranquilizers.

"That pill," Dr. Ching said, "is their only contact with reality." Immediately they retreated within themselves. There was silence again.

Suffering is the same, no matter where you live or

what language you speak. As we left the hospital, I pondered over what I had just witnessed and wondered what was so different about this hospital from the ones at home. The answer eluded me.

When I returned to tell Bill and Helenmarie of the afternoon's experience, it dawned on me that here, in San Salvador, the patients didn't suffer from the smell of uncleanliness. Their rooms were open to the fresh air. The fragrance of flowers wafted over the courtyards. At least this was one blessing they enjoyed.

Our stay in San Salvador was not one of only seeing the ill and handicapped. We visited parks, shops, and markets, where peasants with baskets of eggs or iguanas on their heads came to sell. The flower markets were fragrant with bouquets of jasmine, lilies, roses.

We dined with the Peace Corps personnel and their families, and they wound up our stay with a surprise dinner in our honor, celebrating our wedding anniversary.

The vacation came too swiftly to its end. It was difficult to hold back the tears as we waved good-bye to Helenmarie.

Bill had seemed to weather the visit rather well, but I could sense that he was anxious to be home. We still had a stopover in Mexico to visit the Basilica of Guadalupe, which Bill had always wanted to see.

What a strange experience! Our guide awaited us in the lobby. He spoke fluent English, but he never stopped talking. We were barely on our way when he began charging into us with arguments that we were wasting our time visiting the basilica.

"Just a lot of superstitious people go there," he said. "The Basilica of Guadalupe isn't the most beautiful building in Mexico City. Let me take you on a tour of the ancient ruins, the pyramids, and museums."

There was little doubt that he was an atheist. We were polite but firm. He was downright sullen when we drove into the great square before the basilica.

The square was crowded with schoolchildren, all in line with their teachers supervising them. Our guide parked the car, told us to wait, and walked to the basilica.

"Aha!" he exclaimed gleefully as he returned, "visitors

are not permitted in the church today because special services are being held for schoolchildren.''

"How long?" I asked.

"It will be late this afternoon," he replied. He suggested that he take us on a tour of the pyramids. On our return, we would stop at the basilica.

Somehow the ruins failed to excite us. It was tiring for Bill to walk through them. We had lunch and then instructed our guide to return us to the city. He protested, arguing that we must visit a new museum, but we insisted.

As we neared the city, I could see the dome of the basilica in the distance. At last we would see this holy place. As we motored through the crowded streets, I realized suddenly that we were passing it.

"Stop!" I cried. "We're passing Guadalupe."

"Madame," he replied, "it is late. We should be back at the hotel. Your time is up!"

I answered as patiently as possible. "We hired you to take us to Guadalupe and you promised to return to it. Now, take us there."

He turned the car and headed for the square, which now was overflowing with pilgrims. Some were poor, others rich. Some were natives, many were foreign. Some carried gifts or infants in their arms; some came on crutches or in wheelchairs; some moved on their knees, saying their beads.

It was a moving sight. We wanted to take our time to observe it, but our guide hurried us along to the door of the church.

I was getting thoroughly impatient with him.

We were swept along with the rest of the pilgrims, moving down the aisle. I remember that mass was being offered, but otherwise, I saw nothing in the huge basilica except the picture of Our Lady, high above the main altar.

My eyes were fixed on that picture as we moved slowly down the center aisle. All the while, our guide was chiding us about our superstition and paganism. I cannot remember forming a petition to her—our guide so distracted me—but as we left by a side door, I prayed, "Give me the grace for whatever lies ahead."

We had not been in the church more than five minutes.

Outside, our guide hurried us to the car and returned us to the hotel. We were disappointed, yet, we felt deeply moved by our short stay.

"Did you get a chance to say a prayer?" I asked Bill.

"Yes," he said. "I prayed for Colette."

The next day we flew back to Cleveland.

The following week Bill spent in the hospital, undergoing tests and examinations. For the first time, we were fully confronted with the harsh reality of the change our lives would undergo.

We put off talking about plans for the future, but privately Bill and I were doing a lot of thinking. I was trying to brace myself for the breaking up of our foster family and the rearranging of my life to be mother, father, and breadwinner.

On the seventh day of Bill's hospitalization, I was visiting him when the doctor came. After the usual hellos, the doctor hesitated. Finally he said, "I don't know what you did while you were in Central America, but whatever it was, I suggest you return."

Bill and I looked at each other, bewildered.

The doctor finished, "All the tests and examinations are negative. You can go home, Bill. You are well."

~ 28 ~
Our Lady of the Wayside

It seemed for one brief moment time stopped. There was no past, present, or future. It was as though God lifted us out of reality to listen to Him. Bill spoke first.

"What do you think God is trying to tell us?" he asked.

"Maybe the answer is close before us, and we are too blind to see," I replied.

"What do you mean?" came Bill's question.

"Maybe he wants us to do something for these special children." I really did not know the answer, but the words came from me before I realized it.

"That's the answer," Bill replied, excitement growing in him as the realization of this incredible happening took hold. "Call Tom K—and tell him to begin drawing plans for a house that will take care of thirty-five children." Tom was an architect, and he and his wife, Isabelle, were dear friends dating back to the days of our work at the hospitality house.

It was so very, very good to see Bill bursting with enthusiasm and eager to get to work again. As for myself, I was dazed at the turn of events. Just a few months ago I was hoping and praying to persuade Bill to add an extra room and bathroom, and here we were planning an entire new home.

It was difficult for the children to grasp what had happened. Miracles aren't an everyday happening!

When I had asked Our Lady of Guadalupe for the grace for whatever lies ahead, I surely had never imagined that it would be five years of struggle to raise $250,000 to build a home for special children.

Most of our friends and relatives openly questioned the possibility of two ordinary people, who belonged to the 'payday-to-payday' class, ever raising that amount. Though it was discouraging at times and my patience wore thin, I never doubted that all of the work was part of God's plan.

We soon learned that one cannot just beg for money: good friends soon asked if their gifts were tax exempt. We approached a local attorney who advised us that we would have to incorporate. This we did; according to the laws of Ohio, we became a nonprofit corporation. A friend put us in contact with another attorney who obtained a determination from the Internal Revenue Service that we were a tax-exempt, charitable organization. Now we could beg for the children.

Tom, our architect friend, patiently drew plan after plan for the home, with all the special needs of the children built in. For example, we had been lifting children from the standard bathtub long enough; it was hard on the back. This home would have elevated tubs and special showers with faucets close to the floor; so kids like Todd could take their own showers. Above all, we wanted to build a home, not an institution. We wanted a homelike atmosphere that all children need, with lots of love and security. We wanted it to be bright and colorful—no stainless-steel beds—to bring all the childish joy and wonder to the eyes of these special children. Grays represented institutions in which children are treated like vegetables and respond in the same way. We wanted the home to be alive with the sound of music and filled with toys, pictures, and mobiles; so that little minds and bodies could grow and reach out to a loving world. We wanted large windows and sliding glass doors leading to a patio where wheelchairs and even beds could be wheeled out; so the children could watch the birds build nests and fish splash in the lake. A place where they could see all nature unfold before them each season of the year.

When Tom finished what we hoped would be the final drawings of the new home, we sent copies to the newspapers and also an announcement of an open house. Close friends and neighbors were acquainted with our children—now we wanted the public, near and far, to come and meet them. We wanted friends to see for themselves how beautiful these little ones were and how desperately they needed more room. We wanted to share with them our hopes and dreams of a larger home with plenty of space for play and learning, areas for extra rooms for the children who were on our waiting list.

It was a warm June Sunday when the guests arrived. Our sons and daughters led tours in the house and outdoors, where nature was arrayed in all its lovely, fresh, and lively colors. Under our giant maple tree, beside the lake, we set up tables from which punch and cookies were served to our guests. Indoors we displayed the architect's drawings so that we could point out where each room would be. We mounted pictures of all the children who had been guests in our homes dating back to David.

Our best little hostesses were Susan and Mary, all dressed up in their Sunday best. They invited the visitors to their room and showed them their beds and all their personal treasures. They guided them to the playroom and introduced them to Joey, Steven, Michelle, Charlie Brown, and Tim. They took them to each of the beds and introduced them to baby Marty, Anthony, and Michael. If the enthusiasm of the large crowd could be measured in dollars and cents, we would have had enough money to build our new home that very day. Friends left small gifts and promises to do all they could to help realize the dream house.

One young man wandered from bed to bed and remained a while after the crowd had left. He spent a long time studying the pictures of the children. He was the attorney who had obtained our tax exemption, Oliver S. He said his services would be his contribution to the children. This was quite a gift—we knew the costs of legal sevices and knew vaguely that we would need legal advice often in the months to come.

There were other small donations, but most of all, the enthusiasm and interest of our guests raised our spirits and gave us the encouragement to keep moving ahead.

Gradually we gathered around us a group of friends who dreamed dreams with us. They rallied to the cause of the children and gave their time and service to make the home a reality. Marilyn and John C., whose young handicapped daughter we had cared for on occasion, helped us send letters to friends and foundations begging for money to build a home for God's children.

The first year was spent in planning and getting out letters of appeal. I was so naive; I was sure one or two foundations would be so impressed with our plans that the money would pour in. How disillusioned I became. Good friends responded generously with what they were able to give, but by the end of the second year we had raised only $6,000. We were discouraged and at times wondered if we really were a bit balmy about this whole undertaking.

We applied to state and federal government programs for grants, but were turned down. After three attempts, we put that source out of mind.

By Christmas of the third year, we had $13,000, but inflation was adding to the construction costs faster than the contributions were coming in. Our spirits were low. I had hoped and prayed so desperately for a special Christmas gift, a sizable donation, to get our campaign off the ground.

One evening, Oliver stopped in to go over some legal work with us. "How's the money coming in?" he asked.

"Individuals are giving small gifts, and I am grateful. But what we need are big chunks of money to move ahead," I replied.

Oliver tried to encourage me but I wondered if he, too, was giving up. He walked from bed to bed looking at the sleeping children (we had ten foster children then). He turned to me and said, "I'll see what I can do."

My spirits were as low as the winter skies. January went by and still no sizable donations, just polite responses from various foundations commending us on our worthy cause, but noting their monies were used for other purposes.

Despite this discouragement, I knew that God wanted us to build this home. The reasons for the delay were hidden from us—perhaps it was a testing. We simply had to trust him.

My birthday was coming February 22. Bill planned a

day out to celebrate. My heart wasn't in a festive mood. As I gave the final part to my hair, the phone rang. Eric called "Mom, Oliver wants to talk to you."

We exchanged our hellos and then he said, "I have your first chunk of money." My heart beat faster. He continued, "A good man, a friend of mine who loves children, has pledged $25,000 to our building fund." I don't remember what I replied, for all I could think of was what a birthday present God had sent me. He later brought a business associate of this man to our home who pledged a similar amount.

From that time on the larger chunks of money came in. By fall of that year, the account read $112,000. We now dared to think of breaking ground.

Our enthusiasm was somewhat tempered by the changing economy—prices of materials and labor moved upward almost daily—as our fund rose so did prices. Little butterflies of fear fluttered within us. We called a meeting of the trustees (Oliver, Marilyn, Grace, Dr. Joe, our pediatrician, Anita, Bill, and myself), along with Tom, the architect, and Mr. H., the contractor we hoped would build the home. We studied the plans and cut corners and costs by eliminating the patio and the screened-in porch for the nursery children. The contractor would arrive at a final figure if we would vote to begin immediately. It meant taking out a $90,000 mortgage, which terrified me. His proposal was put to a vote. There was a moment of quiet, tense excitement in the room as the count was taken—the vote was unanimous! We would build the new home. Now all we needed was good weather to put up the shell so the plumbers, electricians, and carpenters could work during the long, cold winter ahead. The children did their share of praying that it would not snow until the roof of our new home was on.

The next day a huge bulldozer lumbered onto the lawn, and almost like a flash, some of our big trees were pushed over like mere twigs. Our lovely cabin, filled with so many happy memories, was reduced to rubble. David carefully picked up the rock and brick and carted them by wheelbarrow back to the meadow, where he vowed to rebuild the cabin.

All of our permits and plans to build had been approved by the local building inspector and officials in our state capital in charge of rules and regulations—or so we thought. To our dismay we learned that a final permit was required from the Water Pollution Control Board in the state capital. There was a building freeze in Avon because the voters had repeatedly rejected sewer installations.

We took our problem to the mayor and begged him to intercede and win an exception for us from the board. After several telephone calls, he was told the city had to make a written application. It would then be taken up at the January or February meeting.

"Impossible!" I cried. "We can't wait until January. The builders must get the shell up before the heavy snows come, or they will be unable to begin until spring, and by that time the price will be higher. We must have a decision at the December meeting."

The mayor held little hope for the earlier presentation, but the planning commission and the council passed the necessary resolutions. The legal papers were drawn, and the mayor wrote a personal letter to the Water Pollution Control board explaining our project and the urgent need for a decision. Oliver made a special trip to the capital so that the papers could be filed with the board in time for consideration at the December meeting.

We were all discouraged, knowing how slowly the wheels of bureaucracy turn. We turned to Mary, Mother of God, again, and pleaded with her to give us another miracle.

December 8th, the day of the meeting, arrived. It dragged on painfully—finally the news arrived—the board agreed that ours was an urgent and exceptional case. Permission was granted to build, provided the proper sewage treatment facilities were installed.

The builders were swept up in the cause of the children. Each day the youngsters stood by the windows with their noses pressed against the glass, watching the workmen put up their new home. Throughout December and January, the weather was mild and sunny, and by the end of January, the roof was on.

Late one afternoon, looking out the window, I saw

one of the workmen climbing a ladder to the roof, carrying a small pine tree on his shoulders. He made his way to the peak of the roof and hoisted the tree to the top. He then nailed braces to tree and roof to hold it in place.

I was puzzled with this strange activity and went outdoors to ask him the meaning. He smiled and said, "It's an old German custom. When a new building is raised, and its roof is in place, we celebrate our success with music, dancing, beer and good food, and place a tree, symbol of life, on the top of the new building."

Whether the workers celebrated that evening, I never discovered, but we celebrated and offered thanks that the weather remained mild and sunny throughout January.

The next day oil heaters were rolled inside to keep the building warm; so the carpenters, plumbers, and electricians could continue their work throughout the winter. As they worked, we paged through catalogs of carpeting and visited furniture stores to pick drapery material. We planned a special color scheme for each room—twenty-eight in all. When we broke ground we had barely enough money to complete the building. Furnishing it was the next hurdle. One friend donated carpeting for the entire building. Others came through with donations of time and money.

The work was moving along smoothly and on schedule. Each evening, after the workmen left, we slipped into the new home and walked from end to end over piles of lumber, pipes, and tools. We pictured in our minds each room's color and which children would be its occupants.

Each day's progress drew cries of delight. Even the smell of the fresh cut lumber increased our excitement and anticipation of the day we would move in.

At this point another bit of excitement was injected into our lives. We were invited to join a pilgrimage of the mentally and physically handicapped to Lourdes, France, to the shrine where the Mother of God appeared to Bernadette Soubirous. At the time it seemed an impossibility for me to leave with all the work to be done as we neared completion of our home. But Bill insisted I take Colette and Todd and join the thousands of physically and mentally handicapped children from all over the world, who would pray and sing and offer thanks at the Grotto of Lourdes.

It was an experience I shall never forget. Twenty thousand pilgrims—many on litters, in chairs, and on foot—some blind, deaf, and mentally retarded—arrived by plane, train, bus, or car at the small town of Lourdes. It was Holy Week; the flowers, tulips and daffodils, had already burst into bloom for spring comes early there.

Unlike other pilgrimages (so we were told by the inhabitants of Lourdes) ours was one of great joy and festivity. The pilgrims crowded the streets and grand esplanade before the shrine, singing songs of praise and joy in their native tongues. Almost every country in the world was represented. The days were planned so that pilgrims from each country had special services. At night there were candlelight processions, which were indescribably beautiful—a weaving sea of tiny flickering lights.

The atmosphere was one of joy and hope, but one could not help observing the weeping parents. For parents there will always be the wound, the deep suffering of having a handicapped child. No amount of resolution ("I will accept this child.") completely erases the pain. For myself I asked the Mother of God for the grace to detach myself from Colette, enough so that I could look upon her as I did my foster children and see only the beautiful girl she was and not be overwhelmed with her handicap.

I'm sure many were praying for miracles of healing. Whether any occurred, I do not know, but I believe many returned home with new faith, light, and courage in looking upon the mystery of why God permits this suffering.

We roamed the narrow winding streets of Lourdes, visiting Bernadette's home and parish church. Todd, Colette, and I made many visits to the shrine and perhaps even knelt on the spot where little Bernadette knelt when the Mother of God first appeared to her.

In the grotto where others left crutches and braces when miracles appeared, we left a small brochure describing our new home. With it we left our thanks for the miracle of Guadalupe.

After a huge fiesta with singing and dancing on the

esplanade on Holy Saturday, followed by celebration of the mass on Easter Sunday, we left for home full of joy, faith, and peace.

The work had piled up at home. With only six weeks left before opening, we worked long into the night.

Adolph, our painter, met me quite distressed one morning, soon after our return. "Madame," he said in his heavy German brogue, "you must have made a mistake with some of the colors you selected. Surely you don't want a room with three orange walls and one white, and another room with three dark blue walls and one white. Let me paint them a nice aqua."

"No, no, Adolph," I replied, "do as I instructed— you'll see what beautiful playrooms they will be after the pictures are on the walls and the drapes are hung."

Aqua indeed! It would look just like a hospital.

Weeks later the orange playroom was transformed into a child's jungle. A young artist friend, Linda, had painted a mural on the white wall of all the happy animals of the forest. The white drapes were printed with a design of brown and green monkeys. The blue playroom was turned into what is known as our red, white, and blue room. It has red and white striped drapes, and the white wall comes alive with circus clowns. Even Adolph admitted we had done a great job of decorating.

At last we dedicated our new home. It was beautiful, nestled among the trees overlooking the lake. It was alive with color and music and filled with friends who had helped to build it for God's children.

Above all, it was filled with the children, who carried their toys and clothes from the old house and put them carefully in the new closets and drawers. Finally, the children cut the red ribbon stretched across the entrance and sent hundreds of balloons heavenward to praise and thank God.

We all called this new home Our Lady of the Wayside.

About the Author

Dorothy Gauchat has dedicated her life to the care of handicapped children. Since her husband, Bill, died early in 1975, she has carried the responsibility of the management of the home that they established in Avon, Ohio, for the care of children with special needs.